"Tell Me a Story"

Developmentally Appropriate Retelling Strategies

JILL HANSEN

Woodfern Elementary School
Hillsborough, New Jersey, USA

INTERNATIONAL
Reading Association
800 BARKSDALE ROAD, PO BOX 8139
NEWARK, DE 19714-8139, USA
www.reading.org

The International Reading Association attempts, through its publications, to provide a forum for a wide spectrum of opinions on reading. This policy permits divergent viewpoints without implying the endorsement of the Association.

Director of Publications   Joan M. Irwin
Editorial Director, Books and Special Projects   Matthew W. Baker
Managing Editor   Shannon T. Fortner
Permissions Editor   Janet S. Parrack
Acquisitions and Communications Coordinator   Corinne M. Mooney
Associate Editor, Books and Special Projects   Sara J. Murphy
Assistant Editor   Charlene M. Nichols
Administrative Assistant   Michele Jester
Senior Editorial Assistant   Tyanna L. Collins
Production Department Manager   Iona Muscella
Supervisor, Electronic Publishing   Anette Schütz
Senior Electronic Publishing Specialist   Cheryl J. Strum
Electronic Publishing Specialist   R. Lynn Harrison
Proofreader   Elizabeth C. Hunt

Project Editor   Charlene M. Nichols

Cover Design   Linda Steere

Photo Credits   Jill Hansen and Marybeth Schwartz

Web addresses in this book were correct as of the publication date but may have become inactive or otherwise modified since that time. If you notice a deactivated or changed Web address, please e-mail books@reading.org with the words "Website Update" in the subject line. In your message, specify the Web link, the book title, and the page number on which the link appears.

Library of Congress Cataloging-in-Publication Data
Hansen, Jill, 1964-
  Tell me a story : developmentally appropriate retelling strategies / Jill Hansen.
      p. cm.
  Includes bibliographical references and index.
  ISBN 0-87207-538-9
  1. Reading comprehension--Study and teaching (Primary) 2. Developmental reading.
I. Title.
  LB1525.7.H36 2004
  372.47--dc22
                                                                                    2004004593

Contents

Introduction

This book is based on my belief that a developmental approach is an effective method of reading instruction in the primary grades. In *Learning to Read and Write: Developmentally Appropriate Practices for Young Children* (International Reading Association [IRA] & National Association for the Education of Young Children [NAEYC], 1998), IRA and NAEYC conclude that learning to read and write requires a wide variety of instructional approaches and goals and expectations for young children that are *developmentally appropriate*, that is, *"challenging but achievable*, with sufficient adult support" (p. 15). Using a developmental approach to teach literacy-related skills helps ensure that a child achieves success with reading tasks because the tasks are appropriate for his or her age and stage of literacy learning. When children succeed in reading at the beginning of their schooling, they develop positive attitudes toward reading and learning that greatly influence their chance of future success in school in all subject areas (Carbo, 1996; Stanovich, 1986). This evidence demonstrates why successful reading experiences in the primary grades are so invaluable to children.

One important step in guiding primary-grade students toward reading success is helping them make meaning from text. According to the National Reading Panel (NRP) report (National Institute of Child Health and Human Development [NICHD], 2000),

> Comprehension is critically important to the development of children's reading skills and therefore their ability to obtain an education. Indeed, reading comprehension has come to be viewed as the "essence of reading" (Durkin, 1993), essential not only to academic learning but to life-long learning. (p. 4-1)

One method of teaching reading comprehension is through retelling a story, which incorporates several of the research-based strategies recommended in the NRP report, such as using graphic organizers, identifying story structure, and summarizing text.

What Is Retelling?

As children read, they have a natural need to share the ideas from the text (Glazer & Brown, 1993). Story retelling develops children's awareness of a story's content and demonstrates their level of reading comprehension (Morrow, 1993). This instructional strategy is simple and effective, and it can be used to assess children's understanding of a story once a teacher has adequately modeled it for them. Retellings are effective assessment tools because "when a child is asked to do a retelling, he or she becomes engaged in tasks requiring use of oral or written language, recall, and comprehension of narrative text" (Heiden, 1999, p. 80). The strategy of retelling also matches the goal of reading—to interact purposefully with all the ideas of the text (Glazer & Brown, 1993).

To begin a retelling, the student is simply asked to retell—either orally or in writing—a story that he or she has read, and then the teacher evaluates the student's understanding of the story by analyzing his or her ability to comprehend and verbalize the story's basic elements: the main character(s), the setting, the problem, the attempts to solve the problem, the solution, and the ending. The teacher also evaluates the student's understanding of the story by assessing whether his or her retelling offers a cohesive and sequentially organized summary of the text.

If a student can effectively retell what he or she has read, the teacher can assume that the student understands the story and is ready for further reading comprehension instruction. For example, a teacher can ask the student inferential and evaluative questions about the story if the student demonstrates a strong understanding of it, whereas the teacher cannot ask these types of questions if the student does not demonstrate such understanding.

Why Is This Book Necessary?

In order for students' retellings to be assessed effectively, teachers need to instruct retelling in such a way that the students can retell what they have read in a logical, sequential manner. Unfortunately, what I discovered in my search for techniques to instruct emergent readers in retellings was that there is not much practical information available on the topic. Although several leading researchers in the field of literacy address the topic of retellings (e.g., Brown & Cambourne, 1987; Glazer & Brown, 1993; Morrow, 1993; Routman, 2000), often their information focuses more on the analysis of the unguided retelling and what can be learned about the reader's understanding of a story rather than how to guide the reader to retell a story. The information I found does not directly address the needs of primary-grade teachers because it does not offer a practical guide to developing guided retelling.

As a reading content specialist from 1990 to 2002, my role was two-fold: I was responsible for providing additional support to at-risk readers and writers in grades 1 through 5, and I was responsible for providing support and training to the teachers of grades 1 through 5 in all facets of literacy instruction. Because the primary-grade (K–2) teachers I worked with were required to assess students' ability to retell a story but lacked a foundation for teaching retellings, I wanted to provide them with tangible activities for using guided retellings with their students. Based on my work with struggling beginning readers, I began to develop tasks and activities designed to lay this foundation at a very rudimentary level. I combined the successes of the developmental approach to literacy instruction with the technique of retelling, and the developmental retelling technique was born.

The Developmental Retelling Technique

For the purposes of this book, *developmental retelling strategies* are those retelling tasks designed to appropriately match the reading level of the individual student. The three developmental levels are emergent, early fluent, and fluent. Chapters 2, 3, and 4 provide further information regarding these levels. The expected level of sophistication of a student's retelling relates directly to his or her developmental level in reading and writing and to the text characteristics of the books being used for reading instruction. In any given grade, the students' reading levels and the reading levels of the texts used for instruction vary; therefore, the instructional activities have to consider these varying levels in order to determine the amount of teacher direction.

In my first- and second-grade reading groups, I began creating and experimenting with various activities designed to build young students' awareness of a story's events, sequence, and elements. I saw these areas as fundamental in building the foundation for retellings. I believe that the foundation for retellings can begin as early as kindergarten; however, because guided reading is not part of the kindergarten literacy curriculum in my school, the instruction needed to be designed for a shared reading lesson. This situation led to the infusion of the activities into shared reading and shared writing as well as guided reading instruction. By incorporating these components in our balanced literacy program, students are able to gain fundamental instruction in retellings prior to first grade, when the teaching of formal guided reading instruction begins in my school. The use of a balanced literacy program allows teachers the flexibility to teach what is appropriate for their students in an ever-changing classroom environment. Spiegel (1999) notes that this flexibility helps to ensure that each student receives a developmentally appropriate education because he or she is viewed as an individual. A more detailed explanation of the various components of the balanced literacy program used in my school can be found in chapter 1.

How Will This Book Help Instruct Teachers in the Developmental Retelling Technique?

The intent of this book is to guide teachers on how to teach the strategies of retelling within a balanced literacy curriculum in a sequential, developmentally appropriate manner. I believe that retellings can be introduced even before students are actually able to read. As students begin to understand the sound–symbol relationship and develop a sense of initial consonant sounds, they can become more involved in the written retelling through the use of interactive writing. Once students show signs of readiness for guided reading instruction, teachers can further develop and refine the retelling strategy. Follow-up and extension activities from both shared and guided reading instruction will lead students to further practice of retelling, which may incorporate guided writing as well. Eventually, students' independent application of retellings will occur, allowing teachers to assess students' independent reading and writing.

Organization of the Book

Chapter 1 provides the hierarchy of developmental retelling tasks and an overview of the developmental sequence of retellings. The overview summarizes teacher modeling and practical student application for each task in the hierarchy. Chapter 1 also includes the Retelling Instructional Focus Chart (see Figure 3, pp. 15–17), a teacher reference that summarizes the retelling focus and graphic organizer corresponding to a particular reading level. Additionally, the chart lists the corresponding book level as identified by Fountas and Pinnell (1999).

Chapters 2 through 4 take a closer look at the developmental retelling tasks as they fit within the broader developmental levels of reading: emergent, early fluent, and fluent. The emergent level retelling tasks focus primarily on event listing and sequencing, in addition to the introduction of the four basic story elements—(1) character, (2) setting, (3) problem, and (4) solution. The early fluent level tasks build on the four basic story elements, including the completion of a written retelling using the Four-Part Story Map (see Appendix A, p. 82). Additionally, this level introduces students to identifying and retelling main events that lead the story's main character from the problem to the solution. Finally, the modeling and guidance of the completion of the Five-Part Story Map (see Appendix B, p. 88), which includes the sequential recall of the events, brings together all the retelling tasks of the early fluent level. Fluent level tasks then refine the retellings by introducing plot summary. Following all steps of the hierarchy, regardless of the developmental level, the chapters demonstrate teacher modeling, student practice, and teacher assessment of oral and written retellings appropriate for each reading level.

Also included in chapters 2 through 4 are detailed descriptions of how to instruct and assess retellings. Student samples of completed graphic organizers and rubrics are included to clarify the developmental retelling techniques.

The three appendixes, one for each developmental reading level, include reproducible graphic organizers, rubrics, and other teacher materials needed during developmental retelling instruction.

Retelling instruction and assessment have become a beneficial part of the literacy instruction in the elementary school where I teach. Many of the beginning readers who I worked with have experienced success with retellings, demonstrating strong story understanding. This book provides primary-grade teachers with developmentally appropriate retelling strategies that will help them facilitate their students' comprehension development in a similar manner. Students' successful experiences with retellings can lay the foundation for successful future literacy experiences.

CHAPTER 1

Overview of Developmental Retellings

One question that teachers should ask is, How do I teach my students to retell a story? As I mentioned in the introduction, the balanced literacy program in place at my school is used to facilitate both students' learning and, with the integration of the hierarchy of developmental retellings, more focused comprehension. I have found that by using the components of this balanced literacy program to instruct retellings, teachers can meet the needs of the various learners in their classrooms.

The Components of a Balanced Literacy Program

The literacy components in my school are divided into two distinct categories: (1) reading and (2) writing. Then, they are further delineated based on the amount of teacher guidance provided during the particular component, ranging from complete teacher control to independent student application, with a gradual lessening of teacher guidance in between. In order of decreasing teacher guidance, the components of the balanced literacy program are as follows:

Read-alouds, the first component, are totally controlled and directed by the teacher. During a read-aloud, the teacher shares a story or other text with either the whole class or small groups of students. The students are solely listeners during this activity, so the teacher can share information with the class without needing to consider the students' reading levels. For read-alouds, teachers should use texts from a variety of genres as well as texts that depict a diverse society. Teachers can read aloud students' favorite texts many times; rereading helps to establish known texts that can be used as a basis for writing and other activities.

Shared reading occurs when the teacher involves the students in the reading process by using a Big Book that all students can see or individual text copies in which all students can follow along. The story selected typically is age appropriate and related to a specific theme being studied; however, the story is not at an instructional level for all students. For some students, the story may be too difficult to read independently, and for other students the story may be too easy. The purpose of shared reading is not to teach students strategies for figuring out unknown text but rather to teach or model for students a new concept or literacy-related skill or to share information or a common experience. In fact, shared reading provides the perfect opportunity for teachers to model many of the foundational retelling tasks without the need for students to read the selection independently.

Shared writing occurs when the teacher and students work together to compose a message or story. The teacher supports the composition process by acting as the scribe. Due to the nature of shared writing, the students' inability to spell conventionally and to clarify spoken thoughts into complete written sentences is not of concern. During shared writing teachers can model the process of using a graphic organizer to complete a written retelling.

Interactive writing is similar to shared writing in the sense that the teacher still guides the written form of the oral message; however, in interactive writing the teacher involves the students in the writing process to the extent that their participation is developmentally appropriate. For example, when the focus of literacy instruction is for students to identify the initial consonant of a spoken word, the teacher can support student practice of this skill while completing a Story Cluster. (A Story Cluster is an idea-gathering graphic organizer meant to connect a central idea to many related ideas or events.) If the lesson revolves around student recall of items or events from a story, the teacher can ask for volunteers to name the items or events and print the initial consonant of each one. During the interactive writing session, the teacher can gradually shift writing control to the students while continuing to provide practice and reinforcement. For more information on interactive writing, see *Interactive Writing: How Language and Literacy Come Together* (McCarrier, Pinnell, & Fountas, 1999).

Guided reading, the heart of reading instruction according to Fountas and Pinnell (1996), focuses on the student as the primary reader. During a guided reading session, the teacher works with a small group of students who use similar reading processes and read similar levels of text with support. After completing a running record, the teacher selects and uses books that are at the students' instructional level and focuses instruction on constructing meaning while using problem-solving strategies to figure out unknown words, deal with tricky sentence structure, and understand new concepts or ideas. The retelling tasks used during guided reading directly match the text characteristics of the books used. For example, an emergent reader should focus on event retelling, an early fluent reader should retell the basic story elements, and the fluent reader should focus on summarizing the plot.

Guided writing, or **writers' workshop**, is the forum in which students write their own texts with teacher guidance. The teacher encourages students to write on their own, using self-initiated topics. The teacher also provides direct instruction in the form of minilessons and conferences; minilessons typically address the needs of the whole class, such as lessons on capitalization or punctuation rules, whereas conferences are held one on one in order to meet the needs of the individual writer. The teacher models the writing process, and then students work through the stages: prewriting, writing a rough draft, revising, editing, publishing a final text, and sharing the text with others.

Independent reading allows students to apply all the literacy skills they have learned without teacher support and to enjoy self-selected texts. Typically, students read on their own or to a partner from a variety of texts. Some independent reading should be from a collection of books at each student's reading level. In addition, students should be encouraged to read student-created books and various poems and charts displayed around the classroom and to reread books used during shared reading sessions.

Independent writing allows students to practice writing, often in journals, without teacher guidance. The resulting texts should be treated by the teacher as each student's best attempt and should not be corrected.

An understanding of the components of this balanced literacy program in relation to the amount of teacher support needed is necessary for understanding the developmental approach to retelling instruction. The component of the balanced literacy program in which retelling occurs directly influences the developmental level of the task. For example, if retelling instruction is to occur early in the school year during a shared reading lesson in a first-grade classroom, it would be appropriate for the teacher to discuss basic story elements because he or she would be providing guidance with the reading of the text and sharing the act of reading with the students. However, if the instruction were occurring with the same class during a guided reading lesson at the same time of year, it would be appropriate for the teacher to use a more simplistic retelling activity involving event recall or listing because of the emphasis that guided reading has on students reading more independently, with teacher guidance when necessary.

The Hierarchy of Developmental Retellings

The rationale behind this book is that students need to be guided on how to complete a logical, cohesive retelling of a text with direct teacher instruction focusing first on how to identify basic story elements and sequence events and then on how to summarize those basic elements. In order to achieve an unguided retelling, emergent and early fluent readers need to learn strategies designed to build their awareness of story structure and the basic elements of a story in a logical sequence. Thus, I created the Hierarchy of Developmental Retellings (see Figure 1). The hierarchy is a visual representation of the sequence of tasks a reader needs to work through in order to achieve a comprehensive retelling. It is broken down into the three developmental reading levels: emergent, early fluent, and fluent. It is important to note that the type of tasks at each level correspond closely with the text characteristics of the books used at each developmental level. For example, if a teacher wants to focus retelling instruction on the basic story elements, he or she should model a story that clearly depicts character, setting, problem, and solution. Regardless of the level of a task on the hierarchy, teachers should model both an oral and written retelling and allow students to practice retellings as they relate to that particular level.

The Overview of the Developmental Sequence of Retellings in Figure 2 directly correlates with and expands on the Hierarchy of Developmental Retellings by highlighting the recommended teacher modeling and expected student outcome for each step in the hierarchy. The overview is designed to provide a quick summary for the entire sequence of retelling strategies. More detailed explanations of teacher modeling, examples of how to integrate activities into a balanced literacy program, and student examples of applying retelling tasks are provided in chapters 2 through 4.

Because retelling activities modeled and practiced during shared reading can vary greatly from the activities modeled and practiced during guided reading, the developmental hierarchy becomes important for guiding the focus of literacy instruction. Higher-level tasks, based on the Hierarchy of Developmental Retellings, can be taught during shared reading because the act of reading is shared by the teacher and students. Therefore, the characteristics of texts used in shared reading can be more sophisticated than the characteristics of texts used during guided reading. During guided reading, the student takes more responsibility for the act of reading, so the retelling task should become more simplified in nature.

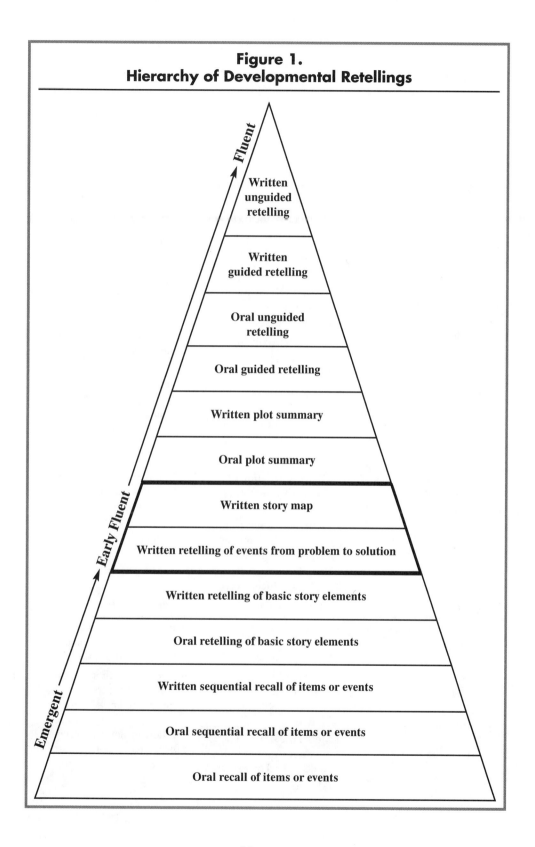

Figure 1.
Hierarchy of Developmental Retellings

Fluent

Written unguided retelling

Written guided retelling

Oral unguided retelling

Oral guided retelling

Written plot summary

Oral plot summary

Early Fluent

Written story map

Written retelling of events from problem to solution

Written retelling of basic story elements

Oral retelling of basic story elements

Written sequential recall of items or events

Oral sequential recall of items or events

Emergent

Oral recall of items or events

Figure 2.
Overview of the Developmental Sequence of Retelling

Emergent Level

Retelling Task	Teacher Modeling	Student Outcome
Oral recall of items or events	• Model completion of Story Cluster	• Participates in oral completion of Story Cluster
Oral sequential recall of items or events	• Number items on cluster to illustrate sequence • Model pictorial event map	• Creates a picture event map illustrating sequential order of story
Written sequential recall of items or events	• Model use of inventive spelling to complete Story Cluster	• Completes Story Cluster or Event Map using pictures or words to represent events in order
Oral retelling of basic story elements (character, setting, problem, and solution)	• Introduce story elements terminology • Display terms in classroom • Model identifying four basic story parts • Model completion of Four-Part Story Map • Model use of Four-Part Story Map to guide oral retelling	• Participates in oral discussions and uses story element cards, demonstrating understanding of basic story elements • Practices guided oral retelling using completed Four-Part Story Map
Written retelling of basic story elements	• Model completion of Four-Part Story Map during shared reading • Model use of Four-Part Story Map to complete simple written retelling	• Completes Four-Part Story Map as a shared reading follow-up • Completes a simple six-sentence written retelling

Early Fluent Level

Retelling Task	Teacher Modeling	Student Outcome
Written retelling of events from problem to solution	• Model oral and written identification of events leading from problem through solution • Model completion of Problem-to-Solution Event Map • Model use of Problem-to-Solution Event Map to guide an oral or written retelling	• Practices oral and written completion of Problem-to-Solution Event Map • Recites Retelling Poem and demonstrates understanding of story elements through various follow-up activities such as group discussions and art projects

(continued)

Figure 2. (continued)
Overview of the Developmental Sequence of Retelling

Early Fluent Level (continued)

Retelling Task	Teacher Modeling	Student Outcome
Written story map	• Model language of retelling; teach Retelling Poem • Model completion of Five-Part Story Map during follow-up discussion of shared reading • Model use of Five-Part Story Map to guide an oral or written retelling	• Learns poem and demonstrates understanding of story elements • Completes Five-Part Story Map • Completes an oral or written retelling using the Five-Part Story Map

Fluent Level

Retelling Task	Direct Teaching	Student Outcome
Oral plot summary	• Model identifying the main character's attempts to reach his or her goal using four questions: 1. What is the character's goal and what is the obstacle that stands in the way of achieving it? (Goal/Obstacle) 2. What are the attempts to reach this goal and the outcome of each attempt? (Episodes) 3. What is the outcome of the final attempt? (Resolution) 4. What does the character do or feel about the outcome? (Ending) • Model completion of Plot Summary Map	• Engages in oral discussions designed to demonstrate understanding of story plot during shared or guided reading • Participates in oral completion of Plot Summary Map
Written plot summary	• Model how to compose a paragraph answering the questions above	• Writes a paragraph incorporating the answers to the plot summary questions

(continued)

Figure 2. (continued)
Overview of the Developmental Sequence of Retelling

	Fluent Level (continued)	
Retelling Task	*Direct Teaching*	*Student Outcome*
Oral guided retelling	• Model oral retelling using the Five-Part Story Map and/or story board created during shared or guided reading	• Participates in oral retelling activities during shared or guided reading using previously developed Plot Summary Map or story board
Oral unguided retelling	• Demonstrate thinking strategy necessary to recall main story elements needed to create a concise unguided retelling	• Gives an unguided retelling one on one, in a small group, with the whole group, or independently into a tape recorder
Written guided retelling	• Model paragraph design using a complete story map for guidance (use interactive approach to involve students) • Chart and display model for student reference (color code or label story elements)	• Completes a written guided retelling
Written unguided retelling	• Model thinking strategy necessary to prepare for a written unguided retelling (involve students in activities designed to develop short, concise retellings)	• Completes a written unguided retelling

Determining the Instructional Focus
for Developmental Retellings

Because the tasks that are developmentally appropriate for students during shared reading may vary greatly from the tasks used during guided reading for some students in the same grade, the amount of teacher support provided, in addition to the text level and its correspondence to each student's reading level, determines what tasks students can be expected to accomplish successfully. In order to guide teachers on which task to teach based on their students' reading levels, I created the Retelling Instructional Focus Chart (see Figure 3), which directly correlates the appropriate retelling focus with the reading level used during shared reading or with the letter level of texts (as assigned by Fountas & Pinnell, 1999) used during guided reading. For example, when a first-grade teacher uses the chart at the beginning of the school year to plan instruction for a student reading at the emergent instructional level of C/D, the retelling focus during guided reading is to model and guide oral and written retelling strategies relating to event listing and sequencing either using a story cluster to collect ideas or event boxes to retell events in sequential order. However, if the same first-grade teacher is developing a shared reading lesson to use during a whole-class session at the same time of the school year, the chart would guide the instructor a bit differently. In this situation, the teacher could model retelling tasks relating to the oral and/or written identification of the basic story elements, completion of the Four-Part Story Map, and the use of the Four-Part Story Map to retell a story both orally and in written form. These tasks are more developmentally appropriate for the beginning of first grade during shared reading, as opposed to during guided reading, because the story line in the text can be more sophisticated when the student and teacher are sharing the act of reading. The text characteristics and higher level of story development of the books used during shared reading lead to a more natural forum for discussing the basic story elements such as character, setting, problem, and solution. Additionally, the written tasks involved would be more appropriate for a shared writing lesson during which the teacher could act as the scribe.

Figure 3.
Retelling Instructional Focus Chart

Reading Level	Letter Level	Retelling Focus	Graphic Organizer
Readiness	A, B	Model oral recall of items and events	Story Cluster
Preprimer	C	Model and guide oral and written recall of items and events in sequential order	Story Cluster with items numbered

(continued)

Figure 3. (continued)
Retelling Instructional Focus Chart

Reading Level	Letter Level	Retelling Focus	Graphic Organizer
Preprimer	D, E	Model and guide written recall of items and events in sequential order	Event Map
Primer (first part of grade 1)	F, G	Model and guide oral and written identification of basic story elements (character, setting, problem, solution)	Four-Part Story Map
Grade 1	H, I	Model and guide oral and written events leading from problem to solution	Problem-to-Solution Event Map
		Model and guide oral and written retelling using Four-Part Story Map	Four-Part Story Map
Grade 2 (first half)	J	Model and guide written Five-Part Story Map with events from problem to solution	Five-Part Story Map
		Model and guide oral and written retelling using Five-Part Story Map as a prompt	Retelling Rubric/ Checklist
Grade 2 (second half)	K, L	Independent completion of Five-Part Story Map	Five-Part Story Map
		Guide oral and written retelling using story map	Retelling Rubric/ Checklist
Grade 3 (first half)	M	Model and guide basic elements of plot summary	Plot Summary Map
		Guide oral and written retelling using independently completed story map	Five-Part Story Map Retelling Rubric/ Checklist
Grade 3 (second half)	N, O	Complete Plot Summary Map independently	Plot Summary Map
		Model and guide oral and written retelling using Plot Summary Map or Plot Summary Response Sheet	Plot Summary Map Plot Summary Response Sheet
Grade 4 (first half)	P, Q	Guide oral and written retelling incorporating elements of Plot Summary Map or Plot Summary Response Sheet	Plot Summary Map Plot Summary Response Sheet Retelling Rubric/ Checklist

(continued)

Figure 3. (continued)
Retelling Instructional Focus Chart

Reading Level	Letter Level	Retelling Focus	Graphic Organizer
Grade 4 (second half)	R, S	Complete written plot summary independently using Plot Summary Map or Plot Summary Response Sheet	Plot Summary Map Plot Summary Response Sheet
Grade 5	T, U	Complete an oral and written retelling independently using Advanced Story Map	Advanced Story Map Plot Summary Response Sheet

Note: Reading letter levels based on Fountas and Pinnell's Guided Reading book levels.

By using the balanced literacy components described in this chapter as a basis for teaching developmentally appropriate retelling tasks, students will experience great success in developing concise, unguided retellings.

CHAPTER 2

Emergent Retelling Level

I n 1966, New Zealand researcher Marie Clay introduced the term *emergent literacy* to describe the behaviors of young children when they use books and writing materials to imitate reading and writing activities. *Emergent readers* are readers who are just beginning to realize the wonders of the printed word. They are beginning to understand that by putting letters together in a certain way, they convey a message. Some children grasp the relation between letters and sounds quickly, while others learn at a slower pace. Emergent readers are beginning to demonstrate one-to-one correspondence—the ability to match the spoken word with the word in print. Emergent readers use pictures to support meaning, and they rely on language as a strong cueing system (Fountas & Pinnell, 1996).

Teachers can nurture emergent readers' development through modeling and direct guidance during the shared reading and writing components of a balanced literacy program. The emergent level retelling tasks are designed to lay the foundation for unguided retellings. Many of the tasks can be modeled by teachers and practiced and applied by students prior to the introduction of formal guided reading instruction. This eliminates the need to delay the direct teaching of the retelling tasks until students have mastered the act of reading. During this stage of students' literacy development, teachers begin to move from using shared reading experiences to more guided experiences that focus instruction on helping students independently read texts. Therefore, texts at the emergent level should be easy and familiar to students. Typically, Fountas and Pinnell's book levels A–E are used for instruction during guided reading.

Students at this stage of literacy development enjoy storytelling. Teachers often overhear emergent readers retelling favorite stories as they "read" independently. The process of retelling a story draws from the young student's book sense, book handling skills, knowledge of the function and purpose of print, and understanding of the story line (Heiden, 1999). At this reading level, students are already setting the stage for comprehension building on their own.

As emergent readers start to read independently, the use of retellings will help keep both the readers and their teacher focused on meaning making. It is easy to see how as emergent readers struggle to decode words, the sense of story may become lost. However, if students know that a retelling will be expected from them after reading, they will know to focus their energies on the meaning of the story as well.

The emergent level retelling tasks include the first five tasks on the Hierarchy of Developmental Retellings. The tasks included in this early stage focus on listing items or events as well as sequencing them and identifying the basic story elements. These retelling tasks are designed to match the text characteristics of many of the stories used in the early primary grades.

In this chapter, expanded information on teacher modeling and instruction and student application is provided for each developmental retelling task, along with concrete examples to further clarify the intended student outcomes. Possible assessment uses for retellings are also included.

Pyramid diagram, from top (Fluent) to bottom (Emergent):

- Fluent
- Written unguided retelling
- Written guided retelling
- Oral unguided retelling
- Oral guided retelling
- Written plot summary
- Oral plot summary
- Written story map
- Written retelling of events from problem to solution
- Early Fluent
- Written retelling of basic story elements
- Oral retelling of basic story elements
- Written sequential recall of items or events
- Oral sequential recall of items or events
- Oral recall of items or events
- Emergent

Oral Recall of Items or Events

The first retelling task introduces emergent readers to the world of comprehension using oral language. Children who struggle as writers may not be able to express their understanding of stories in writing as effectively as they can orally (Heiden, 1999). However, as students are instructed on how to listen and/or read a story, they can simultaneously be instructed on how to orally retell story events or items in order to demonstrate basic story understanding.

Teacher Modeling and Instruction

Prior to primary-grade students actually being able to read, literacy instruction primarily involves teachers spending a great deal of time and energy modeling the practices of reading and writing. Shared reading and writing lessons provide natural settings for teachers to guide oral discussions designed for student recall of the main items or events mentioned in a story. These discussions are the beginning of comprehension instruction.

Many of the books used during shared reading at the emergent level have similar text characteristics. They tend to be repetitive, provide strong picture clues to match the items or events listed, use rhyme patterns, and have simplistic story lines. It is easy for emergent readers to successfully recall items or events from these books because the meaning of the story is often so readily understood.

The oral recall of items and events can be modeled by teachers and practiced by their students during shared reading lessons using these types of books (see p. 40 for recommended titles). As is true with many emergent level books used during shared reading, the catchy phrasing often becomes ingrained in the minds of young readers. Teachers can then capitalize on the ease with which students can remember the stories by instructing students in ways to retell what they have learned through listening to stories and reading along.

After an initial introduction to a story and several readings of the text, the students can be asked to retell the story by providing oral responses while the teacher completes a Story Cluster (see Appendix A, p. 74, for a reproducible Story Cluster). The Story Cluster can be simple, or it can artistically reflect the topic or theme of the story. For example, when reading a book about animals on a farm, you can use a sketch of a barn as a Story Cluster.

Because teachers model the gathering of written ideas for students, students can participate in a retelling without having complete knowledge of sound–symbol correspondences and spelling conventions. Teachers simply pose questions designed to have the students recall the items or events, and then the teachers act as the scribes to record the student responses.

An Example of Oral Recall of Items or Events

After several readings of *There's a Dragon in My Wagon* (Nelson, 1989), I used the Story Cluster to challenge my first-grade students to try to recall all the people the young girl in the book encounters while pulling her wagon through town. I did not allow the students to refer to the book; however, I did give them one last opportunity to reread the story before beginning the recall activity. By allowing the reread, I promoted the students' success; the students became so familiar with the story that they could readily accept the challenge of recalling characters with confidence. After I asked the students, "Who did the little girl meet while pulling her wagon?" I recorded each character the students recalled and wrote their names on the Story Cluster (see Figure 4A and B). After the students were confident that they had recalled all the characters, we reread the text to confirm each response.

To add to this activity, teachers can model the think-aloud strategy of stretching out the words being written on the Story Cluster to isolate their initial consonant sounds and other common sounds such as *at* or *ing*.

Teachers also can further involve students by having them place a check mark on the Story Cluster next to each response as it is reread from the book, matching the text from the story to writing on the Story Cluster.

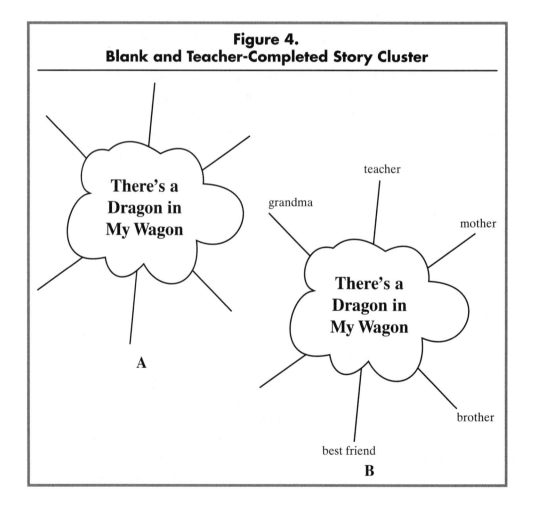

Figure 4.
Blank and Teacher-Completed Story Cluster

Student Practice and Application

After several lessons modeling this type of recall of items or events, teachers should give students their own Story Clusters and encourage them to complete the clusters using pictures or symbols either in small groups, pairs, or independently. Teachers can challenge students further by asking them to use inventive spelling, attempting at least the correct initial consonant sound for each word. For example, Figure 5 is a Story Cluster completed by a kindergarten student after reading *Colors* (Sloan & Sloan, 1996).

Assessment

The oral recall of items or events is students' first retelling task. Although it is meant to be an introductory task, it reveals the level of understanding an emergent reader is able to verbalize. Teachers can use a blank Story Cluster to record students' oral responses (see Appendix A, p. 74, for a reproducible Story Cluster that can be used for recording purposes) and later analyze the responses to determine information such as how quickly students recalled the information, if medial events were missing, and so forth. Teachers can use this information to tailor instruction to their students' needs.

In order to determine a quantitative score, divide the number of items or events recalled by the student by the total number of items or

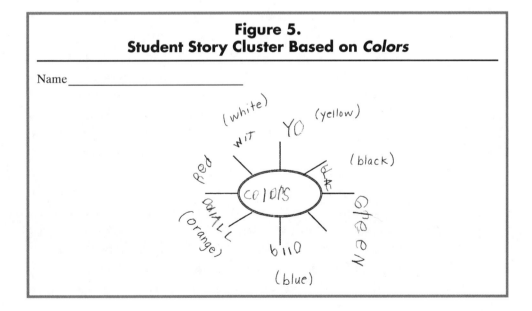

Figure 5.
Student Story Cluster Based on *Colors*

events in the story. For example, if there were 8 events in a story and the reader recalled 6, divide 6 by 8 and multiply by 100 to determine that 75% of the events were recalled.

Oral Sequential Recall of Items or Events

The oral sequential recall of items or events builds on the students' familiarity with oral recall by asking them to retell the story in the order in which it occurs in the book. Again, beginning with shared reading activities, teachers should have students focus their attention on the order in which the items or events are stated within the text. Sometimes, the items or events are not arranged in a purposeful order; if so, the sequential recall is a simple memory-building type of activity. At other times, the sequence of events is very important in carrying the message of the story to the reader. In the latter case, students' true comprehension development can begin. The emergent readers should be asked to consider what they already know about the story topic to help guide their sequential recall of events and to question if their recall is logical, based on this knowledge.

Teacher Modeling and Instruction

To teach oral sequential recall, the teacher can revisit the Story Cluster created to initially record the recalled items or events from a familiar story. By doing so, the focus of the lesson will be the sequencing of items or events, rather than the introduction of a new story. If, however, a teacher chooses to use a new story for this activity, he or she should only introduce the oral sequential recall task after several shared readings of the story.

Prior to rereading this familiar story, the teacher should inform the students that they will be reading the story for the purpose of recalling the events in the order in which they happen. After rereading the text, the teacher should challenge the students to number the items already charted on the Story Cluster in the order in which they occur in the story. If the story is new to the students, the teacher can combine the two tasks of recall and sequencing by encouraging the students to recall the events in order to create a new story cluster. The teacher should always verify the accuracy of the attempts by rereading the book with the students, confirming their attempts, and correcting any inaccuracies.

The oral sequential recall task can be further modeled by the teacher and practiced by the students as a follow-up during guided reading. Many emergent reading level books lend themselves perfectly to this type of activity. Continual teacher modeling of and student practice with these books will reinforce students' sequencing skills.

An Example of Oral Sequential Recall of Items or Events

The children's book *Pumpkin, Pumpkin* (Titherington, 1986) discusses the steps from planting a pumpkin through the final carving of a jack-o'-lantern. By using students' prior knowledge, in this case of planting and growing, teachers can tap a valuable resource to aid the students' recall of events. The sequencing of these events must have a logical order. Students can understand that you have to plant the pumpkin seed first before you can have a flower appear on the pumpkin vine. The task of sequencing the events can be modeled in a variety of ways.

One activity that helps emergent readers learn how to arrange events in order involves using picture cards that correspond with the text. The teacher makes simple picture representations of the main events of the story. Then, students can manipulate the cards to illustrate the sequence of the story's events (see Figure 6). By using pictures, rather than text, even a nonreader can demonstrate the ability to recall a story in sequential order after a shared reading lesson.

Figure 6.
Students Arranging Picture Cards

Initially, this can be done as a whole-group lesson in which students are randomly selected to hold a card and then decide how to arrange themselves in a line to correctly represent the story. In addition, students can be introduced to transitional words or ordinal number words and asked to match these words with the pictures. For example, *first* the pumpkinseed was planted, *second* the seed sprouted, *third* the plant began to grow, or *first* the seed was planted, *then* the seed sprouted, *next* the plant began to grow.

After completion of either sequencing activity, the teacher should begin to model how to retell the story using the picture cards. Teacher modeling will begin to reinforce students' speaking skills as well as demonstrate the understanding of the sequential recall of the events needed to retell a story. The students who did not actively participate in the activity by holding cards can be asked to verify the sequence of the story by listening to an oral retelling given by the teacher and supported by the picture prompts.

Student Practice and Application

Following shared reading lessons, students should be continually challenged to orally retell events in order. Students can work with a partner, in small groups, or independently on placing picture cards in the appropriate order. Students can also orally retell events in order as a follow-up to guided reading lessons.

Assessment

Teachers can keep anecdotal records to note individual students' ability to orally retell a story in order. Again, by recording this information on a simple Story Cluster, teachers can see growth in students' ability at this task. The reproducible Story Cluster in Appendix A (p. 74) can be used for recording purposes; teachers can use the cluster to record the student's name, the book title, the date the book was read, and the date the book was retold. In addition, during individual student conferences, teachers can assemble portfolios consisting of audiotapes of students' oral sequential retellings that can be shared with parents to demonstrate their children's literacy growth over time.

Written Sequential Recall of Items or Events

Once the foundation for sequential recall of a story's main items or events has been laid, students should be ready to apply the strategy in written form. Children's writing skills develop rapidly during the emergent stage of literacy development, and encouraging their use of writing in conjunction with the retelling tasks provides them with writing practice and helps to develop their skill in phonetic spelling. During written sequential recall, it is appropriate and beneficial for students to apply phonetic knowledge to invent spellings to label pictures. Emergent writers are beginning to realize that writing letters and words is essential for producing a message that someone else can read. As students progress within this level, they are learning much about letters and sounds. When working with emergent writers, an important goal is to help them make beginning connections between their own oral language and the graphic symbols that represent language (McCarrier, Pinnell, & Fountas, 2000).

Teacher Modeling and Instruction

Written sequential recall can be taught using either pictures or words, depending on the student's level of writing development. Using pictures helps emergent readers with the rereading of the recall (Johnson, 1999). When moving from the use of pictures to the use of words, teachers should encourage students to identify initial consonant sounds first, then gradually encourage them to use phonetic spelling until they learn conventional spelling. The modeling of this task should begin during shared reading and shared writing lessons. After the reading of a book in a shared reading lesson, the teacher can begin a discussion of the sequence of events in the story; however, this time the teacher also should create a written list or visual representation of the events as recalled orally by the students.

Teachers should continue modeling written sequential recall during shared reading and shared writing lessons, incorporating the use of interactive writing as much as possible. Students will be much more willing to write when they have practiced the task during a shared reading or writing lesson. After several lessons modeling this task, teachers can use extension activities stemming from both a shared reading lesson and a guided reading lesson using one of the event maps in Appendix A (pp. 75–79). The student examples in Figures 7, 8, and 9 provide models of the final products that students are capable of completing once ample modeling and practice have been provided.

Figure 7.
Event Map Completed With Pictures

Name _____

Book Title A Tree Fell Over the River

Use pictures or words to retell the events of the story in the correct order.

Event 1 m	Event 2 C	Event 3 S

Event 4 D	Event 5 W	Event 6 B

Figure 8.
Event Map Completed With Words

Name _____

Book Title A Tree Fell over The River

Use pictures or words to retell the events of the story in the correct order.

Event 1	Event 2	Event 3
Masst	Lkinmokk	skock

Event 4	Event 5	Event 6
Dtieer	WuFe	baar

Figure 9.
Event Map Completed With Pictures and Words

At the Farm

tractor → cow → goat → sheep

horse → duck → pig

An Example of Written Sequential Recall of Items or Events

Using a storyboard is an easy, fun introduction to the written sequential recall. A storyboard is a visual representation of a story's sequence of main events. It can be completed by the whole class, in small groups, in pairs, or individually.

The introduction of the task should be modeled initially to the whole class to ensure all students' understanding of written sequential recall of events. Next, the teacher should demonstrate the task and allow students to practice it in small groups or independently with a developmentally appropriate text. Once the students' lists of items or events are confirmed to be accurate, the students each should be assigned one item or event from the list to illustrate. When the illustrations are complete, the whole class should discuss them and decide on the order in which to display them. Then, the teacher should guide the children in creating a large storyboard depicting the items or events of the story in proper sequence. The class should revisit the storyboard and the teacher should use it to guide an oral retelling of the story.

For example, after reading *The Jacket I Wear in the Snow* (Neitzel, 1989) with a small group of first-grade students, I guided a discussion recalling the items of clothing that the main character put on to go out in the snow. As the students recalled the items of clothing, I recorded the responses on a chart. Then, I challenged the students to arrange laminated pictures of the items of clothing in the proper sequence. As a group, we did a quick rereading of the text to verify the accuracy of the sequential recall. Next, I assigned each student a different item of clothing to illustrate. Finally, the students pasted the clothing items in the correct sequence onto a large sheet of butcher paper to create a storyboard that retold the story in sequential order through illustrations (see Figure 10). I modeled and then guided an oral retelling using the storyboard as a prompt. The oral retelling included the title of the story, a brief introduction, a sequential listing of events, and a concluding statement.

To reinforce students' skills in oral sequential recall, teachers should continually model the task, using illustrations as prompts.

Figure 10.
Sample Storyboard

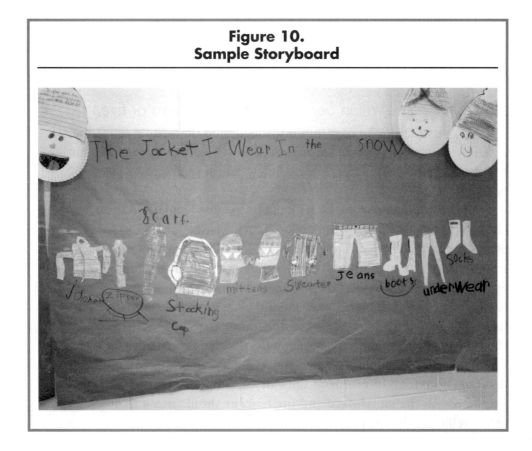

Student Practice and Application

As follow-up work to both shared and guided reading lessons, students can use any of the event maps provided in Appendix A (see pp. 75–79) to create class, small-group, or individual storyboards that show the sequence of events in a story. The continual reinforcement of this strategy will ensure students' eventual success in spontaneously recalling a story in sequential order.

Assessment

Once students have practiced oral sequential recall in shared reading lessons, teachers can use this task as an assessment tool. An independently completed event map—using either invented spelling or illustrations—can be used to assess a student's ability to comprehend a story. In fact, "The ability of emergent readers to gain meaning from picture cues is an important indicator of their level of reading development" (Heiden, 1999, p. 81).

Although running records, such as *An Observational Survey of Early Literacy Achievement* (Clay, 1993) used in my school district, provide valuable information regarding students' accuracy rates, strategies used to decipher unknown text, and self-monitoring strategies, they do not provide information about the students' ability to understand the story. Teachers can easily obtain information revealing students' understanding of the story, the order of items or events, and the overall theme by using any of the retelling strategies mentioned thus far in addition to a running record. Students can complete graphic organizers as independent writing activities, and then teachers can analyze students' ability to recall the events and the order in which the events were told. Teachers also can use students' completed work to get an idea of students' ability to connect written phonemes to spoken words.

Oral Retelling of Basic Story Elements

As students' literacy skills continue to develop, the stories that teachers use during shared reading and guided reading should become more sophisticated. Text selection should change gradually so that the repetitive pattern needed to guide emergent readers is replaced by simple story lines that usually include a problem and solution. Sentences should be longer and, although illustrations are still needed to support the text, the focus shifts from the illustrations to the text.

Because the natural inclination for emergent readers is to retell every detail of a story, it is important for teachers to instruct them on how to convey the most important components of a story in order to give a concise retelling. Teaching this task is invaluable and vital for classroom management purposes as well.

Teacher Modeling and Instruction

Teachers should begin by introducing the basic story element terms—*character*, *setting*, *problem*, and *solution*—and modeling how to identify them. Teachers should use the terms naturally when discussing a story during shared reading. Teachers can talk about how characters are animals or people. Teachers can explain *setting* in terms of where and when a story takes place. Because the element of time is abstract, it is often difficult for students to understand. Teachers can discuss time in connection with the seasons, days of the week, or morning and night because these concepts will be familiar to students. However, the concept of past, present, or future is not relevant for students at this level and should not be addressed. Teachers can help students understand that the story's problem needs to relate to the story's main character and that every story has a problem that is ultimately resolved. Teachers and students should discuss the solution to the problem: Was the character satisfied with the solution? If not, what did the character do, or how did he or she feel?

These basic ideas should be incorporated into shared writing activities as well. By modeling how to identify basic story elements, students will develop oral retellings that each have a beginning, middle, and end. Again, the key to success with this task is repeated modeling. Teachers should be sure to display the story element terms around their classrooms and encourage students' use of the terms when describing a story. Teachers also should ask students many questions as follow-ups to both shared and guided reading lessons, encouraging students to demonstrate their understanding of the basic story elements. Eventually, the task can be guided for independent application.

An Example of Oral Retelling of Basic Story Elements

One activity designed for student practice, and for eventual teacher assessment of students' understanding of the four basic story elements, uses cards with the story element terms printed on them or picture symbols representing character, setting, problem, and solution (see Appendix A, pp. 80–81, for reproducible story element cards). I gave each student in my first-grade class a set of cards and asked all the students to hold up the appropriate card in response to a statement one of them gave during a follow-up discussion of a familiar story. The class had read *A Kiss for Little Bear* (Minarik, 1968). I said, "Hen, cat and skunk" and then asked the students to hold up the card that identified the story element mentioned. The students held up the character card. I continued by stating, "Hen said there was too much kissing." The students held up the problem card. I continued giving statements that provided examples of all the story elements in a similar manner.

This activity could be done during a whole-class shared reading lesson or a small-group guided reading lesson (see Figure 11 for an example of cards being used during a small-group guided reading lesson). The benefit of this activity is that it gives all students an opportunity to be active participants. The activity also could be reversed. The teacher could hold up a story element card and ask students to provide examples from the text that match the story element on the card.

Figure 11.
Students Working With Story Element Cards

Student Practice and Application

Teachers should provide opportunities for small-group practice of this task during follow-up discussions to guided reading lessons. Teachers can encourage students to think about the story that they just read by discussing the importance of the setting. In addition, teachers can have students identify the characters and their problems and can guide students to relate the characters' problems to their lives. This rich discussion, centering on the basic story elements, will help students gain meaning from the text. Gradually, students' use of the basic story element terms will become natural when they discuss stories. Using the Four-Part Story Map (Appendix A, p. 82) will help students organize their information about the character, setting, problem, and solution, and students can use the story map to guide their oral retelling.

Assessment

The goal of this task is for students to orally identify and retell the basic story elements—character, setting, problem, and solution. Therefore, observational or anecdotal reports provide teachers with the best information regarding each student's understanding and ability to orally identify story elements and retell a story.

The Oral Retelling Rubric (Appendix A, p. 83) or a teacher-created checklist can provide a quick record-keeping system of student progress (see Figure 12 for a completed rubric). By keeping a systematic checklist on each student, the teacher can see a student's performance at a glance. The teacher also can record a student's strengths and weaknesses to evaluate student learning. For example, the checklist may show that a student usually does not identify the story's setting. In this case, the teacher can redirect or focus instruction on that specific weakness to develop the student's ability in this area.

Written Retelling of Basic Story Elements

The written retelling of basic story elements demonstrates students' understanding of the task modeled during instruction of the oral retelling of the story elements. Teacher modeling and student application of this task are developed in two steps. The first step involves the transfer of the oral identification of the basic story elements into written form on the Four-Part Story Map, and the second step involves the use of the story map to compile a simple six-sentence retelling of the basic story elements.

Figure 12.
Completed Oral Retelling Rubric

Name 1st grade student

(✓ each story element mentioned while student is orally retelling a story.)

Date: 10/6   10/30   11/7   11/21

	10/6	10/30	11/7	11/21
Character	✓	✓	✓	✓
Setting	? needed prompting	where ✓	prompt when	✓
Problem	✓	✓	✓	✓
Solution	?	✓	✓	✓

Notes:

10/6 Needed clarification of term setting. Solution didn't connect with problem.

10/30 Knew setting - where Prompted when - unsure

11/7 Prompt (when) setting

11/21 Clearly identified all basic elements

Teacher Modeling and Instruction

Teachers should introduce this task as a follow-up to a shared reading lesson. Teachers should first model how to complete the Four-Part Story Map (see Appendix A, p. 82) during shared and guided writing lessons. Or, they can create their own story map on chart paper, an overhead transparency, or the chalkboard. Each of the four boxes should be labeled with one of the story element terms—*character*, *setting*, *problem*, and *solution*. After a shared reading of a story that clearly illustrates each element, teachers should guide students through the process of orally identifying text or picture clues demonstrating each element. Then, using pictures or words, teachers can model how to complete the story map.

Next, the Four-Part Story Map can be used to model a simple written retelling, the second step to the written retelling task. As a follow-up to a shared reading lesson in which the story map was completed, teachers can use a shared writing lesson to model a written retelling. They should encourage students to assist in the completion of an opening sentence that includes the title and author of the book. Then, teachers should guide the development of a sentence for each component of the Four-Part Story Map. The result will be a simple six-sentence retelling.

An Example of Written Retelling of Basic Story Elements

After a guided reading of *Washing Our Dog* (Lang, 1996), I asked my first-grade students to reread the story and answer questions designed to identify the characters, setting, problem, and solution. As they provided the answers using the text, I modeled how to complete the story map on chart paper. Because this was the first time we had completed such an activity, I then allowed the students to use the completed chart to guide them through the independent completion of the Four-Part Story Map. They were allowed to fill in the map with either pictures, words, or both (see Figure 13A and B). By providing a model, I eliminated the stress of students needing to independently identify the story elements as well as complete the story map. As an introductory lesson to the story map, I simply wanted to familiarize students with how to complete the map.

On the next day, I used the students' completed story maps to model how to compose a simple written retelling. Again, the goal was to demonstrate the steps of transferring information from the story maps into sentence form. Teachers need to provide much guidance and many opportunities for student practice at this stage before leaving students to complete this task independently.

Student Practice and Application

In subsequent lessons, the two tasks—identifying the story elements and completing the Four-Part Story Map—should be combined. However, teachers need to provide sufficient modeling first. The students' success with the activity will be highly dependent on the modeling provided. Teachers should encourage student involvement by using interactive writing during a

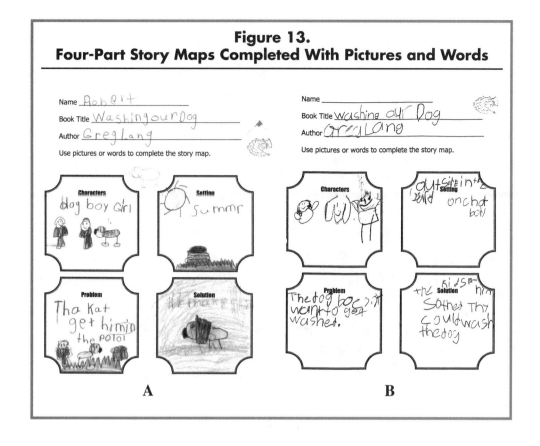

Figure 13.
Four-Part Story Maps Completed With Pictures and Words

Name Robert
Book Title Washing our Dog
Author Greg Lang

Use pictures or words to complete the story map.

Characters
dog boy Girl

Setting
summr

Problem
Tha Kat
get himin
the Potol

Solution

A

Name
Book Title washing our Dog
Author Greg Lang

Use pictures or words to complete the story map.

Characters

Setting
outSite in the
yeld   onchot
        bov

Problem
The dog does'n
wean to get
washed.

Solution
the kids po him
Sothed Thy
could wash
the dog

B

whole-class or small-group lesson. By doing this, the transition to the independent application of the task will be smooth, thus making students feel confident and capable of performing the activity without teacher direction.

Teachers can introduce the Four-Part Story Map as a prewriting tool for organizing story ideas during guided writing and also incorporate its use as a graphic organizer in writers' workshop. This task transposes itself into a natural framework for story development including all the basic elements needed for a logical piece of writing.

After one first-grade guided reading group completed *Mr. McCready's Cleaning Day* (Shilling, 1997), I guided them to complete the Four-Part Story Map (see Figure 14). Then, I guided them in the completion of a written retelling using the story map as a prompt (see Figure 15).

Assessment

After teacher modeling and student practice, teachers can use students' individual applications of the task for assessment purposes. For record

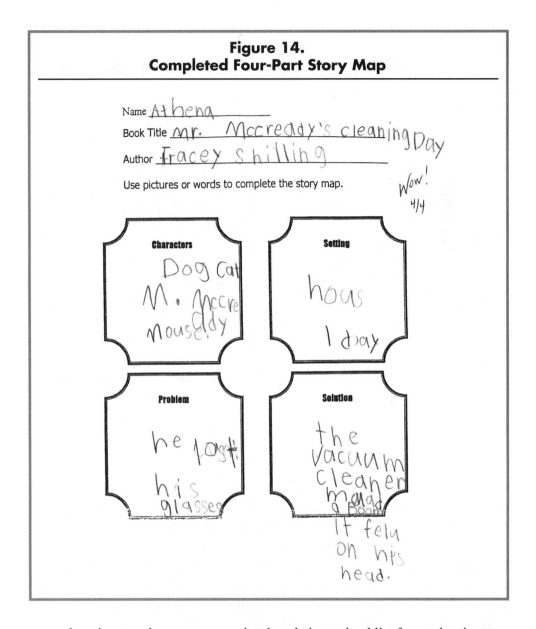

Figure 14.
Completed Four-Part Story Map

Name _Athena_

Book Title _Mr. Mccready's cleaning Day_

Author _Tracey shilling_

Use pictures or words to complete the story map.

Wow!
_4/4_

Characters

Dog Cat
M. Mccre
mouse dy

Setting

hous

1 day

Problem

he lost
his
glasses

Solution

the
vacuum
cleaner
and
a Book
It felu
on his
head.

keeping, teachers can use a simple rubric or checklist for evaluating students' oral or written retellings based on the Four-Part Story Map. For the lesson on *Mr. McCready's Cleaning Day*, I used the Oral and Written Retelling Rubric to analyze each group member's work (see Figure 16).

As stated in the beginning of this chapter, the emergent level retelling tasks are necessary in order to build a firm foundation for clear, concise retellings. As evidenced by the many examples provided, ample teacher modeling and student practice and application need to occur for students'

Figure 15.
Sample Written Retelling

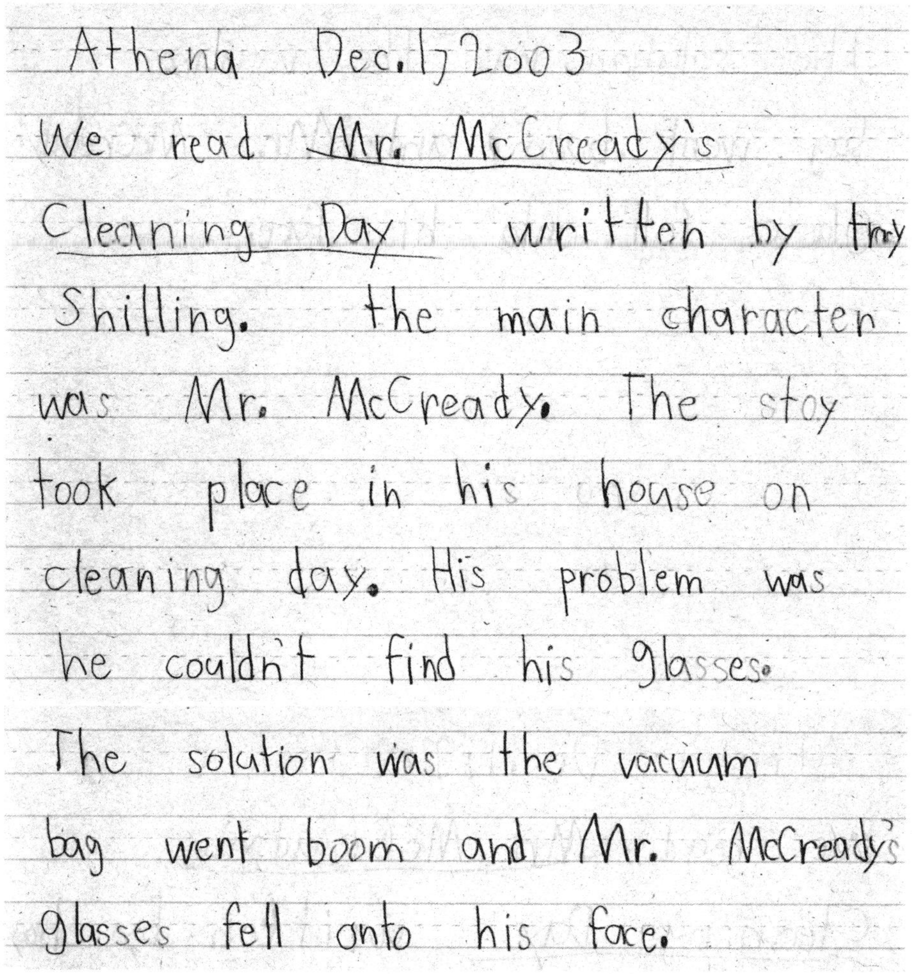

> Athena Dec. 17 2003
>
> We read *Mr. McCready's*
> *Cleaning Day* written by tny
> Shilling. the main character
> was Mr. McCready. The stoy
> took place in his house on
> cleaning day. His problem was
> he couldn't find his glasses.
> The solution was the vacuum
> bag went boom and Mr. McCready's
> glasses fell onto his face.

progression to the next retelling task. The emergent level retelling tasks cannot be rushed, or skipped altogether, even if a teacher has students who read at higher levels and with greater fluency than the rest of the class. Comprehension instruction, focusing on the basic story elements and sequential manner in which they occur, is a necessary and vital part of students' further understanding of stories and development of retellings. The focus of every kindergarten and first-grade classroom should be on modeling these basic retelling tasks. The next level of literacy development, the early fluent level, will build on the knowledge and understanding of the emergent level tasks.

Figure 16.
Completed Oral and Written Retelling Rubric

Student Name __Athena Zinn__   Date _____

Book Title __Mr. McCready's Cleaning Day__

Author __Tracey Shilling__

Indicate yes or no for each story element mentioned. Score 1 point for each element fully identified.

Story Element	Score
Character(s) __yes__	__4/4 (1)__ (#characters/total #)
Setting: Where __yes__	__1__
When __yes__	__1__
Problem __yes__	__1__
Solution __yes__	__1__
Total score	__5/5__

Comments:

All story elements clearly verbalized. Even mentioned secondary characters & time on story map. Written retell was completed with guidance on how to use story map.

Additional Titles to Use for Modeling and Practicing Emergent Level Retelling Tasks

Carle, E. (1969). *The very hungry caterpillar*. New York: Putnam.

Carle, E. (1991). *A house for hermit crab*. New York: Simon & Schuster.

Hillman, J. (1989). *Goldilocks and the three bears*. Crystal Lake, IL: Rigby.

Martin, B. (1983). *Brown bear, brown bear, what do you see?* Ill. E. Carle. New York: Henry Holt.

Raffi. (1998). *Wheels on the bus* (Raffi songs to read). Ill. S. Wickstrom. New York: Crown.

Taback, S. (1997). *There was an old lady who swallowed a fly*. New York: Viking.

CHAPTER 3

Early Fluent Retelling Level

E arly fluent readers understand the basic rules of how to decode a printed message. They recognize a large number of frequently used words on sight and use pictures in a limited way while reading (Johnson, 1999). Early fluent readers also are slowly moving from simple word calling (reading words without thinking of the meaning) to reading (making meaning from the printed word). They are beginning to understand that these simple words make up a story in a logical way. Because of this, the early fluent reader will begin to question the text, making certain it makes sense. Self-monitoring (asking oneself if what was just read makes sense) that leads to self-correction if inaccuracies occur also is a trait of an early fluent reader (Cutting, 1992). During this stage of literacy development, readers are really learning about what makes sense in a story. With this in mind, it is logical that the early fluent level retelling tasks expand on the emergent level retelling tasks that focus primarily on the recall of events and the introduction of the basic story elements. At the early fluent level, readers learn to apply the sequential event listing to the main character's path from problem to solution.

The books used at the early fluent level tend to contain more detailed story lines than emergent level books (see p. 52 for a list of recommended books). They typically begin with a brief introduction to the main character and setting, then introduce the problem, and follow with several events leading the main character to a solution. These books tend to have more meaning-based events, rather than simple lists of events such as those found in the emergent level texts. Fountas and Pinnell's book levels F–J are appropriate for guided reading instruction at the early fluent level.

The retelling tasks relating to early fluent level stories reflect the texts' higher level of complexity. As Heiden (1999) notes, "The elements asked for in a retelling should parallel those elements of story that are considered appropriate for children to learn at a given grade level" (p. 84). The early fluent level tasks are the next two tasks on the Hierarchy of Developmental Retellings, and they set the stage for the fluent level tasks.

Fluent

Written unguided retelling

Written guided retelling

Oral unguided retelling

Oral guided retelling

Written plot summary

Oral plot summary

Written story map

Written retelling of events from problem to solution

Written retelling of basic story elements

Oral retelling of basic story elements

Written sequential recall of items or events

Oral sequential recall of items or events

Oral recall of items or events

Early Fluent

Emergent

The graphic organizers used at this level are designed to help students visualize the sequence of events that the main character experiences in an attempt to find a solution to his or her problem. In addition, both graphic organizers discussed in this chapter—the Problem-to-Solution Event Map and the Five-Part Story Map (see Appendix B, pp. 86 and 88, for repro-ducibles)—provide opportunities for teacher modeling and student practice of both oral and written retellings. Again, teacher modeling and student practice during shared reading lessons benefit students' transfer and application of this knowledge to guided reading lessons, during which further refinement of the retelling tasks and comprehension develop-ment can occur. Following the proper modeling and practice during both shared and guided reading lessons, stu-dents will be able to demonstrate independent application of the retelling tasks, the results of which teachers can use for assessment purposes.

Written Retelling of Events From Problem to Solution

During the early fluent stage of literacy development, teachers must make sure that students have a clear understanding of what an event is—an action that leads the story's main character from a problem to solution. Expanding on the main character's attempts to resolve his or her problem is then the focus of the early fluent level retelling tasks. Once readers can identify the four basic story elements—character, setting, problem, solution—they can revisit the oral and written sequential recall of events, identify the events that lead the main character from the problem to a solution, and incorpo-rate this information into a more complete retelling. Teachers need to model this task and allow for student practice prior to asking students to complete a Five-Part Story Map, give a complete oral or written retelling of events from problem to solution, or both.

Teacher Modeling and Instruction

Teachers need to follow several steps to teach students this task. First, students need to practice identifying the major story events. During shared or guided reading, teachers can add an event card to the basic story element cards that reinforce students' identification of character, setting, problem, and solution. The same procedure used at the emergent level can be revisited: Either the teacher or the students can make statements relating to a familiar story, and then the teacher can ask the students to hold up the story element or event card that correlates with the statement (see Figure 17 for an example of students using event cards).

To begin reinforcing students' written identification of the events leading the main character from problem to solution, teachers should

Figure 17.
Students Using Event Cards

model completion of the Problem-to-Solution Event Map (see Appendix B, p. 86, for a reproducible copy). Teachers can take advantage of shared reading time to provide direct instruction on this task. As a follow-up to reading a familiar story, teachers can encourage students to discuss the story's problem, events, and solution to guide the written completion of the event map. Teachers can incorporate interactive writing into this activity, having students assist in the completion of the event map by using either pictures or words.

An Example of a Written Retelling of Events From Problem to Solution

As in the written sequential retelling of items or events that is presented in chapter 2, one activity for introducing the written retelling of events from problem to solution uses a storyboard with pictures to depict the problem, main events, and solution. For example, after reading *The Old Man's Mitten: A Ukrainian Tale* (Pollock, 1994), I guided a discussion of the story that began with the students identifying the story's problem—an old man drops his mitten while walking in the snow. Then, the discussion focused on the events in the proper sequence, which involved the animals that encounter the lost mitten and climb into it for warmth. Finally, we discussed the solution of the problem—the old man eventually returns to retrieve his lost mitten. After the oral retelling, I asked the students to name the animals in the order in which they encounter the lost mitten and I recorded their responses on chart paper. Then, the students quickly reread the story to verify accuracy of their retelling. The students also noticed that the animals increase in size as the story progresses. This observation helped guide the students when putting the animals in the proper sequence. Once we were in agreement about the problem, events, and solution, I assigned the students animals to illustrate. Finally, the students pasted all the illustrations in proper sequence onto paper cutouts of mittens to create a storyboard (see Figure 18). Then, I modeled an oral retelling using the storyboard as a prompt.

Teachers can apply this activity to any story that develops the character's journey from problem through solution with clearly identifiable events.

Student Practice and Application

When teachers use problem-to-solution event listing as an instructional strategy following a guided reading lesson, students are encouraged to

**Figure 18.
Sample Storyboard**

pay attention to the problem, events, and solution during the rereading of the text. When using the Problem-to-Solution Event Map (Appendix B, p. 86) or drawing on chart paper to reproduce the storyboard concept that they saw the teacher model during a shared reading lesson, students can retell the story, either in pictures or words, depicting the main events leading from the problem to the solution. This activity demonstrates for teachers their students' level of story comprehension. Oral retellings also can be shared with a partner, in small groups, or with the whole class to further reinforce the concept of events.

For example, after a guided reading lesson using *How Fire Came to Earth* (Davidson, 1993a), I asked second-grade students in a basic skills reading class to retell the story using the Problem-to-Solution Event Map. As the student sample in Figure 19 shows, John was able to correctly identify the problem of the story, recall all the main events, and identify the solution. The only difficulty he demonstrated was confusion with the order of two medial events. Because the events simply involved the listing of

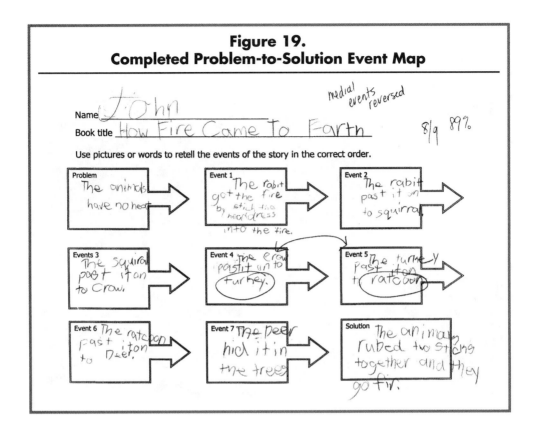

Figure 19.
Completed Problem-to-Solution Event Map

Name *John*

medial events reversed

Book title *How Fire Came To Earth*

8/9   89%

Use pictures or words to retell the events of the story in the correct order.

Problem
The animals have no heat

Event 1
The rabit got the fire by stick the headdress into the fire.

Event 2
The rabit past it on to squirral

Events 3
The squiral past it on to Crow.

Event 4
The crow past it on to turkey.

Event 5
The turkey past it on to ratcoon

Event 6
The ratcoon past iton to Deer.

Event 7
The Deer hid it in the tree

Solution
The animal rubed two sticks together and they go fir.

animals passing fire from one to another, with no logic to the event order, John's error was not as important as an omission or misidentification of the problem, event, or solution. Therefore, I determined that John demonstrated adequate story comprehension for the early fluent reading level.

Assessment

When using this strategy for assessment purposes, teachers should let the students know in advance the number of main events that they are expected to identify because the number may vary from story to story. Then, teachers should simply analyze the event list provided by each student and compare it to the number of main events the student was expected to identify. This assessment gives teachers a clear picture of each student's ability to identify the story problem, sequentially retell the events, and demonstrate understanding of the story's solution. It also provides concrete data for teachers to give to parents regarding their children's abilities to comprehend written material. Figure 20 shows a completed Problem-to-

Figure 20.
Completed Problem-to-Solution Rubric

Student Name _____ Date _____

Story Title How Fire Came To Earth

Score one point for each story element included.

Problem   1/1

Events in sequence   6/7
(# recalled/total #)

Solution   1/1

Total score/remarks: 8/9
        89%

- medial events reversed. (All event recalled)
- not a significant meaning-based error.

Solution Rubric, based on John's completed Problem-to-Solution Event Map from Figure 19. This rubric can be adapted easily for any story (see Appendix B, p. 87, for a reproducible rubric).

Written Story Map

The foundation necessary for students to complete the Five-Part Story Map (see Appendix B, p. 88, for a reproducible copy) has been built step by step through all the previously introduced retelling tasks. By this point, teachers have modeled all the story elements, and students have had opportunities to practice identifying the story elements in shared reading and shared writing activities. In addition, students should have demonstrated under-standing of the retelling tasks by applying them during extension activities in shared and guided reading lessons. Now, students can bring these story elements together on the Five-Part Story Map; they should be able to iden-tify all the basic story elements, incorporate the sequential listing of events, and guide the main character from problem to solution.

Teacher Modeling and Instruction

The text characteristics common to the type of texts used at the early fluent reading level naturally lend themselves to completing story maps because they consist of a problem, multiple attempts by the main character at solv-ing the problem, a solution to the problem, and an ending. With teacher guidance, students should be able to easily identify all the information nec-essary for completing the Five-Part Story Map. To assist students with the recall of the story elements and the sequential order, two first-grade teach-ers wrote the Retelling Poem (see Appendix B, p. 89, for a reproducible copy), which they teach to their students to remind them of the important elements of a retelling. This poem particularly helps students who are auditory learners.

When you read a story

It has more than only one part.

Title, author, introduction,

Are just a few to start.

Setting, character, problems,

And events

Are parts of a story, too.

Solution and ending finish it up.

Let me retell this story to you!

In addition to continual modeling, teachers can use the Retelling Poem and other bulletin board displays as continual reminders of the story ele-ments that students needed to include on their story maps. I also use the Retelling Rainbow (Appendix B, p. 90) or related visual displays that list the story elements (see Figure 21A, B, and C) so students who are visual learners always have a point of reference in the room while they are com-pleting a story map. When modeling a written retelling based on the story map, I also match the color ink with the story element corresponding to it

Figure 21.
Sample Story Element Displays

on the rainbow. For example, the title and author are written in red, characters and setting are written in orange, the problem is written in yellow, and so forth. This color-coding helps the visual learner make the connection with the terms easier, just as the learning of the Retelling Poem helps the auditory learner. These techniques help embed in students' minds the language necessary for retelling.

An Example of a Written Story Map

I began teaching the Five-Part Story Map by modeling its completion during a shared reading and writing lesson. I involved students as much as possible through interactive writing. Because most of the students were having little difficulty representing consonant sounds with letters, with my support they were able to assist in completing the story map. For this modeling process, I have found it helpful to create an enlarged version of the story map and laminate it so corrections can be erased and the story map can be reused.

Student Practice and Application

Students are ready to independently complete a Five-Part Story Map as a follow-up to shared or guided reading lessons once it appears that they can effortlessly identify all the story elements, including the events. The more students practice the identification of the story elements and the completion of the story map, the easier and more natural the skill of retelling a story will be for them. Figure 22 shows a Five-Part Story Map (in the shape of a lighthouse) successfully completed by a second-grade student as a follow-up to a shared reading lesson.

Assessment

Once students can independently identify the story elements and complete the Five-Part Story Map, teachers can use the story map for assessment purposes, in addition to using it as instructional tool to guide students' understanding of a story. The easiest way for teachers to score this type of retelling is to assign a number of points to each story element box and obtain a raw score. For a percentage, the number of items recalled should be divided by the total number of items the student was expected to identify. Figure 23 shows a completed Story Elements Rubric (see Appendix B, p. 91, for a reproducible rubric).

Figure 22.
Five-Part Story Map Lighthouse

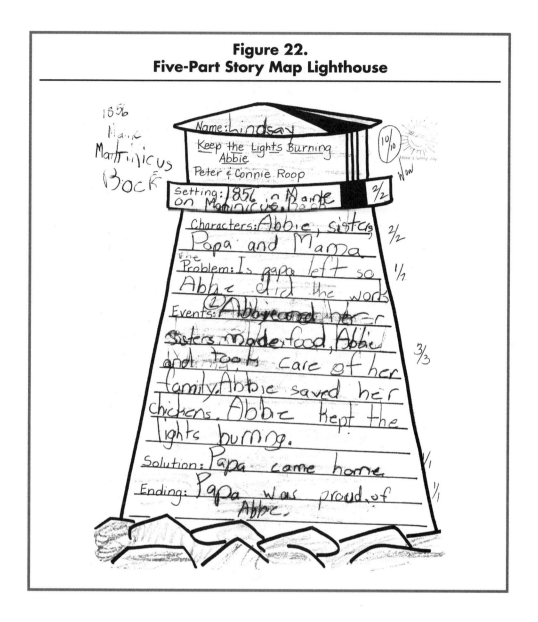

The early fluent level retelling tasks expand on the emergent level retelling tasks by combining the sequential event listing with the retelling of the basic story elements. By merging these two previously learned tasks, the early fluent reader can retell a lengthier story by focusing on the major events leading the main character to resolution of his or her problem. The sequential skill building of these retelling tasks leads students to the fluent level of literacy development. If the foundation has been built properly, the final level of fluent retelling should be a natural progression.

Figure 23.
Completed Story Elements Rubric

Student Name _____ Date _____

Story Title _Keep the Lights Burning Abbie_

Score one point for each story element included.

Setting: Where   _1_
             When   _1_

Characters: Main   _1_
              Others _3/3 = 1_

Problem: _1_

Events: #1 Helped care for family   _1_
        #2 Saved the chickens   _1_
        #3 Kept the lights burning   _1_

Solution: _1_

Ending: _1_

Total score/remarks: _10/10   (100%)_
All elements identified and recalled clearly.

Additional Titles to Use for Modeling and Practicing Early Fluent Level Retelling Tasks

Allard, H.G. (1985). *Miss Nelson is missing*. Ill. J. Marshall. Boston: Houghton Mifflin.

Brett, J. (1997). *The hat*. New York: Putnam.

Cooney, B. (1982). *Miss Rumphius*. New York: Viking.

Freeman, D. (1968). *Corduroy*. New York: Viking.

McDermott, G. (1987). *Anansi the spider: A tale from the Ashanti*. New York: Henry Holt.

McPhail, D. (1988). *The bear's toothache*. Boston: Little, Brown.

CHAPTER 4

Fluent Retelling Level

Fluent readers can read for meaning, with less attention to decoding than early fluent readers, and they can independently solve problems when they encounter unknown text (Johnson, 1999). Fluent readers also can write expressively, using conventional spelling with relative ease. Therefore, teachers can focus literacy instruction for fluent readers on story structure and comprehension development, rather than on strategies for figuring out unknown text.

Fluent level retelling tasks begin with familiarizing students with plot summarizing through story structure instruction. Story structure instruction involves teaching the reader procedures for identifying the content of the story and its plot structure.

> Story structure refers to the finding in discourse analysis that the content of stories is systematically organized into episodes and that the plot of a story is a set of episodes. Knowledge of episodic content...helps the reader understand the who, what, where, when, and why of stories as well as what happened and what was done. (NICHD, p. 4-88)

Although the basic story elements remain the same, the story element terminology changes at this reading level because the texts are longer and sometimes broken into chapters (see p. 70 for recommended titles). With longer texts, teachers should guide fluent readers to look more broadly at the main character's goal, rather than a single problem. Then, teachers should instruct students on how to identify the episodes, resolution, and ending.

Students also need guidance on how to retell a larger piece of writing within a limited amount of space and time. Teachers should model retelling by stating the book title, author, character(s), setting, and plot summary. Teachers should provide opportunities for students to practice this new skill both orally and in writing. Through continued practice, the unguided oral or written retelling will become more natural. Teachers can use the unguided retelling as an invaluable assessment tool to measure students' independent understanding of a story.

Oral Plot Summary

The oral plot summary is a more sophisticated task than simple event listing. By instructing students in how to summarize the plot, they are able to make better choices about which parts of a story to include in their retellings. Because of the range of children's developmental abilities, this is not a task with which students can expect immediate success.

Teacher Modeling and Instruction

The plot elements tie directly to the story elements introduced at the emergent retelling level; however, as previously mentioned, the terminology is different. The problem of the story is now called the main character's *obstacle* because it is what gets in the character's way of achieving his or her goal. The events are now called *episodes*, which include the main character's attempts to achieve his or her goal and the outcomes of each trial to overcome the obstacle. The *resolution* is the outcome of the main character's final attempt. Finally, the *ending* of the story refers to how the character acts or feels in regard to the final outcome.

Teachers must carefully select the stories used to model oral plot summary. Each story should have an easily identifiable goal that the main character wishes to obtain. It also should include several episodes leading the character toward the goal and a clearly stated outcome. Consequently, when teachers model the language of plot summarizing during shared or guided reading lessons, students will easily be able to answer questions about the chosen story. The questions to prompt students' identification of the plot elements are shown in Figure 24. Posting these questions around the classroom can be helpful for students who may need a visual reminder of the terminology.

During shared reading or shared writing lessons, teachers should model how to answer the plot summary questions as complete sentences,

Figure 24.
Plot Summary Elements

Goal/Obstacle

What is the character's goal, and what gets in the way of achieving the goal?

Episodes

How does the character try to reach the goal, and what is the result of each attempt?

Resolution

What is the outcome of the character's final attempt?

Ending

What does the character do or how does the character feel about the outcome?

being sure to restate the question. While eliciting oral responses from students, teachers should chart the answers in sentence form. Writing answers in complete sentences allows students to read back the responses to the questions, thus completing an oral plot summary.

An Example of Oral Plot Summary

After reading *Emma's Problem* (Parker, 1989), I asked students questions designed to elicit the responses necessary to complete a plot summary. I recorded the students' responses on chart paper so that we could reread them word for word. I also modeled how to restate the question when composing an answer.

> Mrs. Hansen: What was Emma's goal, and what got in her way of reaching it?
>
> Student A: She couldn't climb the tree because she was too short.
>
> [Mrs. Hansen writes, *Emma's goal was to climb the tree, but she couldn't even reach the first branch because she was too short*.]
>
> Mrs. Hansen: What was the first thing Emma did to try to reach the branch?
>
> Student B: She tried climbing up a rope, but it broke.
>
> [Mrs. Hansen writes, *First, Emma tried to climb up a rope, but it broke*.]
>
> Mrs. Hansen: So, then what did she do?
>
> Student C: Then, she tried climbing up a ladder, but it fell over.
>
> [Mrs. Hansen writes, *Then, Emma tried climbing a ladder, but it fell over*.]
>
> Mrs. Hansen: What did she do next?
>
> Student B: She tried piling boxes on top of each other, but they fell down.
>
> [Mrs. Hansen writes, *Next, she tried piling boxes on top of each other, but they fell down*.]
>
> Mrs. Hansen: Did she try anything else?
>
> Student A: Yes, she stood on her dog's back, but he ran away when he saw a cat, and she tried bouncing off a trampoline, but she missed the branch.
>
> [Mrs. Hansen writes, *Then, she stood on her dog's back and bounced off a trampoline, but that didn't work either*.]

Mrs. Hansen: Did she ever reach the tree branch?

Student C: Yes, when spring came she got all of the things she had tried before, but when she reached her arm up, she realized that she could reach now.

[Mrs. Hansen writes, *Finally, it was spring again, and Emma got all the things together that she had tried before, but when she reached her arm up, she realized that she could now reach the branch.*]

Mrs. Hansen: How do you think the character felt about reaching her goal?

Student B: Emma felt happy that she could now reach the branch of the tree.

[Mrs. Hansen writes, *Emma felt happy that she could now reach the branch of the tree.*]

Then, I asked the students to read aloud the summary I recorded for them. The plot summary would read as follows:

> Emma's goal was to climb the tree, but she couldn't even reach the first branch because she was too short. First, Emma tried to climb up a rope, but it broke. Then, Emma tried climbing a ladder, but it fell over. Next, she tried piling boxes on top of each other, but they fell down. Then, she stood on her dog's back and bounced off a trampoline, but that didn't work either. Finally, it was spring again, and Emma got all the things together that she had tried before, but when she reached her arm up, she realized that she could now reach the branch. Emma felt happy that she could now reach the branch of the tree.

Student Practice and Application

The underlying purpose of this level of retelling is to have students become familiar with the new terminology of plot summarizing. Through effective teacher modeling, students may appear successful with the new task; however, when students try to demonstrate independent application and understanding of plot summarizing, they may become frustrated. If this is the case, teachers should choose stories with several clear attempts to solve a problem. Several classic tales that work well include *The Three Billy Goats Gruff*, *The Three Little Pigs*, and *The Three Bears*. There are many versions of these stories, and children are usually familiar with their story lines.

The Plot Summary Map (see Appendix C, p. 94, for a reproducible form) should be used as a transitional tool from direct teacher instruction to independent student application of plot summarizing. This graphic organizer serves a dual role: It is an organizational tool that can be used to gather all the relevant information necessary to answer all the questions relating to the plot summary, and it is a prompt for those students still unsure of all the story elements needed. The Plot Summary Map provides a structure that replaces the teacher guidance given to students during the modeling stage. The use of the graphic organizer is beneficial to the reader in constructing meaning and organizing ideas presented in a text. "The external graphic aids (1) help students focus on text structure while reading, (2) provide tools to examine and visually represent textual relationships, and (3) assist in writing well-organized summaries" (NICHD, p. 4-73).

After teacher modeling and student practice of plot summarizing during shared and guided reading and writing lessons, students will be able to identify the plot summary elements and synthesize the information into an oral plot summary without teacher guidance.

Assessment

The oral plot summary can become a valuable assessment tool designed to check students' understanding of a story after a guided or independent reading of a text. Students can share oral plot summaries with the whole class or in small groups. In addition, by using a tape recorder, students can share plot summaries in an independent manner without the need for immediate teacher attention. Teachers can use the Plot Summary Rubric (see Appendix C, p. 95, for a reproducible rubric) to check individual students' story comprehension, and, if desired, they also can use the rubric as a prompt or self-evaluation tool for students.

Written Plot Summary

The written plot summary task simply involves a shift in the responsibility of the writing from teachers to students. The previous task includes modeling for students how to answer the plot summary questions and complete the Plot Summary Map in order to strengthen students' confidence in orally identifying a story's plot. Following the oral plot summary, students should be able to formulate a written plot summary—with the guidance of the Plot Summary Map and the Written Plot Summary organizer (see Appendix C, pp. 96–97, for a reproducible form).

Teacher Modeling and Instruction

The written plot summary follows logically from the modeling of the oral plot summary. Teachers should use the same strategy for modeling written responses to the plot summary questions during shared and interactive writing until they believe the students have internalized the strategy and are ready to apply it independently. As students transition from teacher-directed to independent completion of this task, the prompts on the Written Plot Summary organizer will provide them with questions to guide them in thinking through the strategy of writing a plot summary. However, teachers should continue modeling the formation of a summary paragraph by combining students' responses to plot summary questions, emphasizing the importance of restating the question in the response and using complete sentences.

After students' use of the task appears to have become fairly automatic, they can use the Plot Summary Map to gather notes for completing an oral or written plot summary; this map provides some support without being as time-consuming or laborious as writing out complete statements prior to formulating the plot summary. Teachers should remember that the more modeling they initially provide, the easier students' transition to the independent completion of the task will be.

An Example of a Written Plot Summary

As a follow-up to a guided reading lesson, students in my second-grade class were able to complete the Plot Summary Map and Written Plot Summary organizer with minimal difficulty (see Figures 25 and 26). Then, I used the students' information to model both an oral plot summary and a written plot summary of *Something Soft for Danny Bear* (Broekhuizen, 1990).

Student Practice and Application

Students now need time to practice answering the plot summary questions and responding in writing. The Plot Summary Map will strengthen the students' ability to comprehend and recall story information by providing support in the form of prompts.

Assessment

Teachers can use either the Plot Summary Map or the Written Plot Summary organizer to assess students' understandings of a story and of

Figure 25.
Completed Plot Summary Map

Plot Summary Map #6
Created by Jill Hansen

Plot Summary Map

Character's goal: IS to find something Soft for hibernation

Obstacle: The ground is too bumpy and lumpy

Attempt 1 went to dump - found rocking chair

Outcome 1 too big - gave to mom

Attempt 2 back to dump - found sofa

Outcome 2 too big - gave to papa

Attempt 3 back to dump - found mattres

Outcome 3 Just right

Resolution: Danny sleeps on his soft mattress

Ending: all the bear family are happily sleeping

If additional attempts occur use back of page.

Figure 26.
Sample Written Plot Summary

Name ___Tommy___

Written Plot Summary

Answer the questions below in complete sentences. Then rewrite the answers in paragraph form to complete a written plot summary.

1. What was the character's goal?
   The characters goal was to find something soft for hibernation

2. What gets in the way of the character reaching this goal?
   The lumpy, bumpy ground gets in the way for Danny to hibernatey

3. What was the first attempt?
   first, Danny went to the Dump to look for something soft for hibernation

4. What was the first outcome?
   He found a rocking chair but it was to big so he gave it to mama bear

5. What was the second attempt?
   He went back to the dump this time he found a sofa.

6. What was the second outcome?
   The sofa was to big so he gave it to popa Bear

7. What was the third attempt?
   He went back to the dump for a third time.

(continued)

61

Figure 26. (continued)
Sample Written Plot Summary

8. What was the third outcome? (continue with additional attempts/outcomes as needed prior to #9)

This time he found a mattress it was just right.

9. What was the final attempt and outcome?

Now Danny hibernated on his mattress.

10. What did the character do or feel about the final outcome?

His whole family slept peacefuly

Rewrite the plot summary below by combining your answers.

Danny's goal was to find something soft for hibernation. The lumpy, bumpy ground gets in the way for Danny to sleep. First, Danny went to the dump to look for something soft for hibernation. He found a rocking chair but it was to big so he gave it to mama bear. He went back to the dump this time he found a sofa. The sofa was to big so he gave it to papa. He went back to the dump for a third time. This time he found a mattress it was just right. Now Danny hibernated on his mattress. His whole family slept peacefuly.

how to summarize a plot. When assigning this type of retelling task, teachers should be certain that the chosen text clearly contains all the necessary story elements. In addition, teachers should not predetermine one correct response when assessing students' summaries. Rather, they should read through the entire Plot Summary Map or Written Plot Summary organizer, following the student's understanding of the story, and then determine if it reveals a basic understanding of the story. As long as the plot summary develops logically, teachers should allow for students' individual interpretations.

If teachers desire a quantitative score, they can use the Plot Summary Map or design a simple assessment rubric in which each student response has a point value. Once a raw score has been obtained, dividing the number of correct responses by the number of total possible points and multiplying the result by 100 will provide a percent score. A similar scoring system can be used for the Written Plot Summary organizer. Teachers can assign 10 points to each question; if the story contains more or fewer than three attempts or outcomes, they can adjust the point values according to the number of attempts.

Teachers can make a more valuable assessment by simply reading over a student's written responses and determining if he or she has followed the entire story sequence. Anecdotal records reporting a student's identification of the basic plot summary elements, sequencing of the attempts or outcomes, and general sentence structure also reveal a great deal of information about a student and demonstrate his or her areas of development as both a reader and a writer over time.

Oral Guided and Oral Unguided Retellings

The remaining four tasks on the Hierarchy of Developmental Retellings can be combined by grouping them together by either oral or written form. The growth from the guided retelling to the unguided retelling occurs through independent student application of the task after sufficient teacher modeling and student practice. Once students demonstrate the ability to retell the basic plot of a story, they are ready to give a complete, concise oral retelling by putting together everything they have learned. The oral retelling combines a brief introduction of the story—including the title and author— the basic story elements, and a plot summary. The guidance for the oral retelling can come from a variety of resources—teacher prompting, story maps, classroom posters and/or prompts, or a retelling checklist or rubric.

After teachers slowly decrease the amount of guided student practice, students should be able to complete oral retellings independently.

Teacher Modeling and Instruction

Modeling how to present an oral retelling during postreading discussions—using prompts or graphic organizers—is invaluable. Teacher modeling should focus on all story elements included in the particular retelling checklist or graphic organizer being used. For example, teacher modeling of a story introduction including the title, author, and brief opening statement is necessary if it is included in the grading rubric. If students are expected to include the setting and main characters before the plot summary in a retelling, teachers should demonstrate this sequence beforehand. As students move from guided to unguided and teachers use the oral retellings as assessment tools, teachers should share the grading rubric with their students, possibly even using it as a checklist when students are planning their oral retellings. Students can learn to use any rubric once teachers have modeled the task of oral retelling and given them opportunities to practice it. With a gradual lessening of teacher modeling and prompting, the task should become easier for fluent readers to complete independently.

An Example of Oral Guided Retelling

I began the instruction for an oral guided retelling by leading a discussion on what would be important to tell a third party about a story the students had just read. I asked the students for the following information: the title and author of the story, the main characters and the setting, the goal of the main characters or the basic message of the story, the episodes attempted to reach the goal, and the resolution and ending of the story. I recorded the results from the discussion on the Advanced Story Map (see Appendix C, p. 98, for a reproducible copy). I used the story map as a prompt to guide the oral retelling and later as a checklist for all the story elements.

Once the students understood all the information necessary for a retelling, I guided a second discussion as a follow-up lesson. I modeled how to organize the student responses from the first discussion into simple sentences that, when combined, resulted in a concise, organized retelling. I continually referred the students back to their original responses written on the story map and told them that they should use it as the guide of what to say next.

Student Practice and Application

Following the introduction to this task, teachers should be sure to provide many opportunities for students to practice oral retellings. Small-group discussions as follow-ups to guided reading lessons provide natural opportunities for this student practice. The nonthreatening environment that exists within a small group allows students to continually refine their retelling abilities. Practicing this strategy helps students to develop appropriate speaking skills, which are necessary for a successful oral retelling. Once the students' confidence levels appear to increase, teachers should guide them to complete oral retellings independently.

In addition, discussions as a follow-up to a class read-aloud provide opportunities for teachers to model this more sophisticated task without students needing to be able to read the book on their own at this point in their literacy development.

Assessment

Oral retellings can be assessed using checklists, graphic organizers, or teacher-created rubrics. The assessments can be used as instructional tools for guided retellings and evaluative tools for unguided retellings. They can be easily individualized to match the text being read. The goal is for the student to retell a story in a succinct manner, including all the major points or episodes. A sample scoring rubric is provided in Appendix C (p. 99). However, this Retelling Rubric should be adapted so that the scoring instrument matches the specific characteristics of the text being retold. In addition, teachers can use a tape recorder to record retellings so a student can listen to what he or she said and be involved in scoring or analyzing his or her own retelling. This will allow the student to see what needs to be eliminated from the retelling and what needs to be strengthened. Self-assessment is often more valuable than teacher grading because the student can directly see what needs to be done to improve his or her retelling.

Written Guided and Written Unguided Retelling

The next task is a transfer of the oral retelling into paragraph form. Some students may find this task easier than the oral retelling simply because they are more comfortable writing than speaking; other students may feel the opposite. Again, these two tasks on the Hierarchy of Developmental Retellings are being discussed together because the guided retelling is the instructional part of the task, incorporating the teacher modeling and student practice, whereas the unguided retelling is the independent application that results in authentic assessment of a student's story comprehension.

Teacher Modeling and Instruction

Teachers should model a written guided retelling by recording students' thinking when formulating an oral retelling. The easiest way to guide students' independent application of this task, without much teacher intervention after the initial modeling stage, is to use leading questions. Students may need to review how to answer each question with a complete sentence that incorporates the question within the response. Using the story map created during a guided oral retelling, teachers should record the students' responses. In addition, teachers should model, once again, how to combine the responses to form the retelling in paragraph form, making sure to refer to the retelling rubric to guide the retelling direction and story element inclusion. Finally, teachers should have students practice the task by doing miniretellings on a chapter or two from a chosen story.

Again, another successful prompt to guide written retellings is the Advanced Story Map. Teachers should model note-taking using the story map so that students understand that it can be used to record ideas that can help with their written retellings. It is not necessary for students to complete the story map using complete sentences. Then, teachers should demonstrate the process of using the story map to prompt the responses necessary to complete the written task. Continual teacher modeling and student practice of this activity can lead to a natural process of organizing ideas to create a written unguided retelling.

Student Practice and Application

This task can be practiced after a guided reading lesson, or it can be practiced in a whole-group shared writing lesson after a shared reading. Because teachers have provided continual modeling of retelling tasks, most fluent readers will have no trouble successfully accomplishing a written unguided retelling.

Assessment

When using retellings for assessment purposes, students should be told beforehand that they will be expected to complete a written retelling as a follow-up activity. Then, teachers should direct their students to read the story carefully and think about all the story elements as they do so. After completion of the reading, the students should be asked to complete the Advanced Story Map without referring to the book. Because teachers will use the results of this written retelling to determine if students have a basic understanding of the story, it is important for students to complete this task without referring to the story. Once the students have completed their story maps, they are then asked to complete a written retelling. They should be encouraged to use the map as a prompt to guide their writing.

The retelling also can be assessed using the Retelling Rubric. Teachers simply read over the piece of writing and check off each story element as it is mentioned. If a numerical score is necessary, the teacher can determine a percentage with the rubric. However, the analysis of the written retelling provides a useful glimpse into the student's mind and allows the teacher to truly assess the student's understanding of a story.

Figure 27 shows an example of a story map a second-grade student used as a prompt to guide a written retelling (see Figure 28) of *How Turtle Raced Beaver* (Davidson, 1993b). In addition, Figure 29 shows an example of a scoring rubric used to evaluate the student's performance.

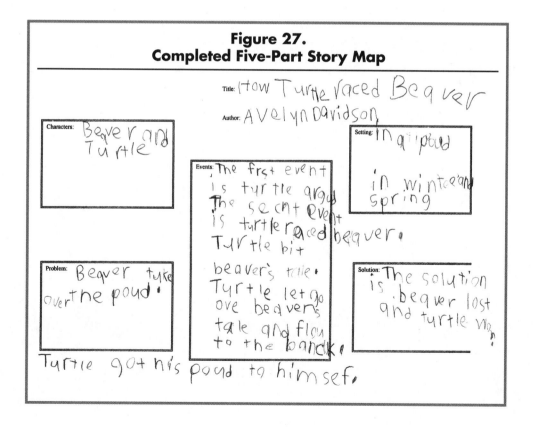

Figure 27.
Completed Five-Part Story Map

Figure 28.
Sample Written Retelling

The title is How Turtle raced
Beaver. The ather of the book
is Avelyn Davidson. The charac
are Turtle and Beaver. The
problem is Beaver tuke
over the poud. The setting
is in a poud in winter and
spring. The frist event is
Turtle argued with Beaver.
The secnt event (idea) is Turtle
raced Beaver. The thred event
is Turtle bit Beaver's
tale. The fourth event is Tut
ftou to the bake. The solution
Is Beaver lost and Turtle
won. The ending is Turtle
got his poud to himself.

Figure 29.
Completed Retelling Rubric

1½ days

Child's Name ___Sal___ Date ___1/25/01___

Title/Author ___How Turtle Raced Beaver___

Type of retelling: (circle one)

Guided (Unguided)   Oral   (Written)

– Indep. completed story map as a prompt

Did the student: Comments

State the title ___✓___

State the author ___✓___

Give an Introduction ___∕___

Describe the setting ___|___
(when & where)

State the characters ___|___

Name all characters? (Yes)/ No

State the problem ___|___

State events in order ___.75___
Events given....

Missing
– Idea to solve problem

Give solution to problem ___|___

Completes the story ___|___ } Well done

Comes to a conclusion/theme ___|___

Score __8.75__ / 10   (88%)

The fluent level retelling tasks call on all that teachers have modeled and students have practiced in regard to retellings. The students are asked to synthesize all that they have learned so far. Graphic organizers guide the retellings, and prior practice with how to retell a story by using graphic organizers as prompts leads to the ultimate goal of an unguided oral or written retelling. Students can achieve this goal if teachers use the developmental approach during the emergent and early fluent reading levels. Once students learn the foundational skill of identifying the story elements, all the additional tasks stem from that skill. The time spent on the retelling tasks building up to the fluent level is as valuable as the result of the unguided retelling, which is a measure of the student's story comprehension.

Additional Titles to Use for Modeling and Practicing Fluent Level Retelling Tasks

Adler, D.A. (2001). *Cam Jansen and the baseball mystery*. Ill. S. Natti. New York: Puffin.

Blume, J. (1978). *Freckle juice*. New York: Yearling.

Cartright, P. (1991). *The fisherman and his wife*. Crystal Lake, IL: Rigby.

Howe, J. (1999). *Pinky and Rex and the spelling bee*. Ill. M. Sweet. New York: Aladdin.

Kline, S. (1998). *Horrible Harry and the ant invasion*. Ill. F. Remkiewicz. New York: Puffin.

Lobel, A. (1979). *Frog and Toad are friends*. New York: HarperCollins.

Osborne, M.P. (1992). *Dinosaurs before dark* (Magic Tree House No. 1). Ill. S. Murdocca. New York: Random House.

Parkes, B. (1990). *Rumpelstiltskin*. Crystal Lake, IL: Rigby.

Concluding Thoughts

The results of the National Reading Panel report (NICHD, 2000) validate the benefits of explicit instruction of comprehension strategies. The Panel's findings support that instruction in comprehension strategies, such as graphic and semantic organizers, story structure, and summarization carried out by classroom teachers who demonstrate, model, or guide readers in their acquisition and use, will lead to independent readers.

Having students retell a story at any developmental level is an excellent strategy for measuring their reading comprehension because it requires the ability to recognize the main character and the sequential steps he or she goes through to resolve a problem or achieve a goal. The tasks discussed in this book help develop the logical framework necessary to organize students' thinking about reading. Whether it is an emergent reader recalling a list of events, an early fluent reader following a character's attempts to solve a problem, or a fluent reader writing an unguided retelling, students now have a framework for story understanding.

Now that the solid foundation of retelling tasks has been developed, step by step, the students' confidence levels and independent applications of the tasks should be apparent. The developmentally appropriate manner in which teachers have taught the retelling tasks will ensure students' well-developed sense of story. In addition, students may start to use the basic story elements in their own story writing, and recall and retell content area materials and events that make up their everyday lives. By teaching the strategy of how to retell a story, teachers will give children a strong foundation for their lives as readers.

Graphic Organizers
for Emergent Retelling Level

Story Cluster

Name _____

Book Title _____

Event Map 1

Name _____

Book Title _____

Directions: Use pictures or words to tell the events of the story in the correct order.

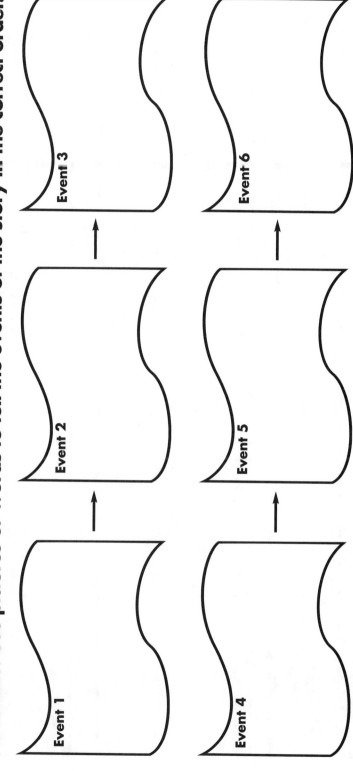

Event 1

Event 2

Event 3

Event 4

Event 5

Event 6

Event Map 2

Name _____

Book Title _____

Directions: Use pictures or words to retell the events of the story in the correct order.

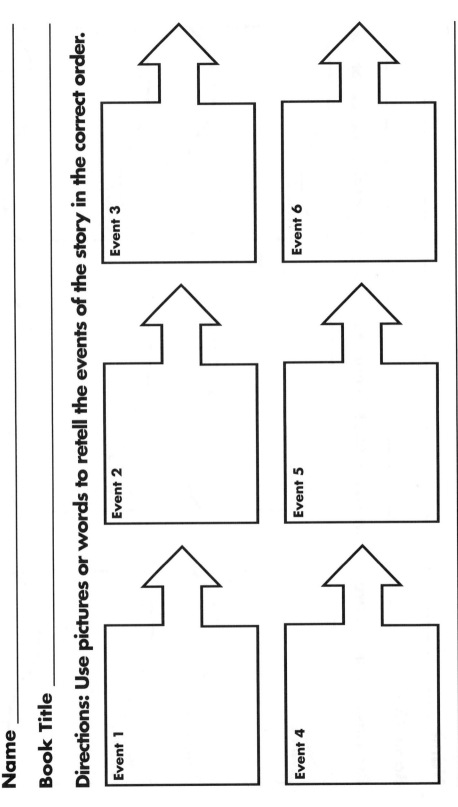

Event 1

Event 2

Event 3

Event 4

Event 5

Event 6

Event Map 3

Name _____

Book Title _____

Directions: Use pictures or words to retell the events of the story in the correct order.

Event 1	Event 2	Event 3

Event 4	Event 5	Event 6

Directions: Place each event on the correct stair to retell the story in the correct order. Begin at the bottom of the staircase and climb up it.

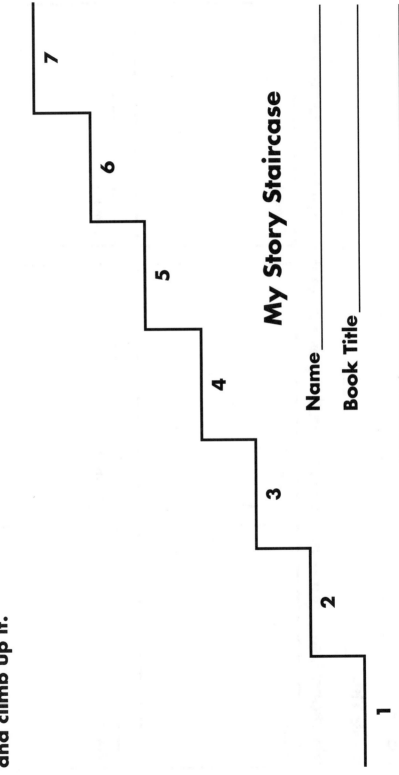

My Story Staircase

Name_____

Book Title_____

"Tell Me a Story": Developmentally Appropriate Retelling Strategies by Jill Hansen. Copyright © 2004 by the International Reading Association. May be copied for classroom use.

My Story Staircase Event Boxes

Directions: Cut out the event boxes and place on the correct step on My Story Staircase to show the order of the story.

Story Element Cards

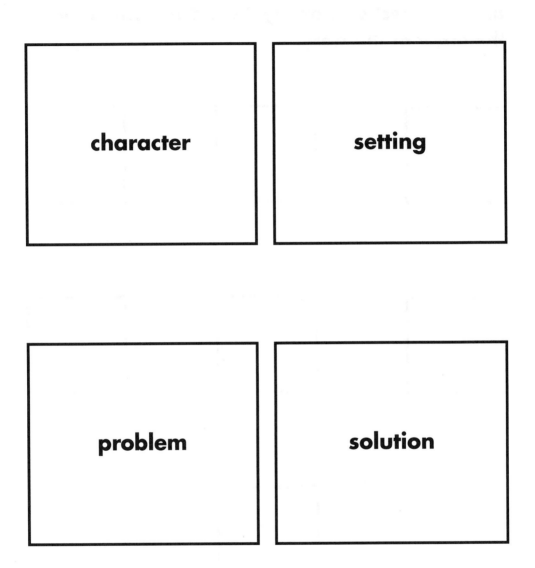

Story Element Cards With Pictures

character

setting

problem

solution

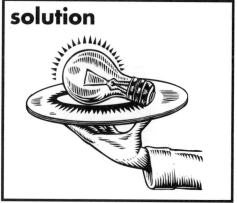

Four-Part Story Map

Name _____

Book Title _____

Author _____

Directions: Use pictures or words to complete the story map.

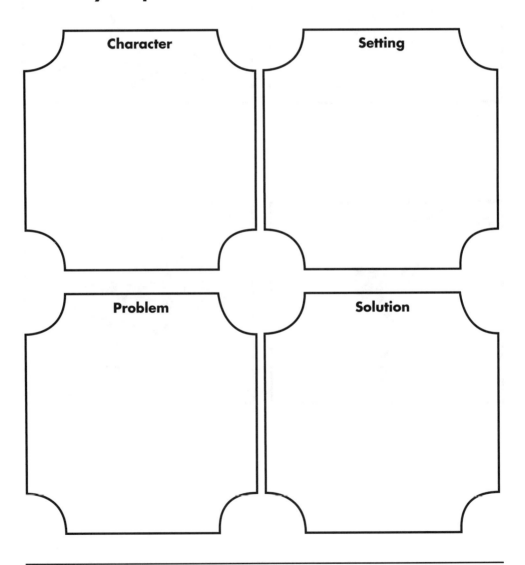

Character

Setting

Problem

Solution

Oral Retelling Rubric

Name _____

Directions: Place a check mark next to each story element as the student orally retells the story.

Dates   _____   _____   _____   _____

Character   _____   _____   _____   _____

Setting   _____   _____   _____   _____

Problem   _____   _____   _____   _____

Solution   _____   _____   _____   _____

Notes:

Oral and Written Retelling Rubric

Name _____

Date _____

Book Title_____

Author _____

Directions: Indicate yes or no for each story element mentioned. Score 1 point for each element fully identified.

Story Element	Score
Character_____	_____
Setting Where_____	_____
When_____	_____
Problem_____	_____
Solution _____	_____
Total Score	_____

Comments:

Graphic Organizers
for Early Fluent Retelling Level

Problem-to-Solution Event Map

Name _____

Book Title _____

Directions: Use pictures or words to retell the events of the story in the correct order.

Problem	Event 1	Event 2
Event 3	Event 4	Event 5
Event 6	Event 7	Solution

Problem-to-Solution Rubric

Name _____ **Date** _____

Book Title _____

Score 1 point for each story element included.

Problem _____

Events in Sequence _____
(# recalled/total #)

Solution _____

Total Score _____

Comments:

Five-Part Story Map

Name _____

Book Title _____

Author _____

Character

Events

Setting

Where

When

Problem

Solution

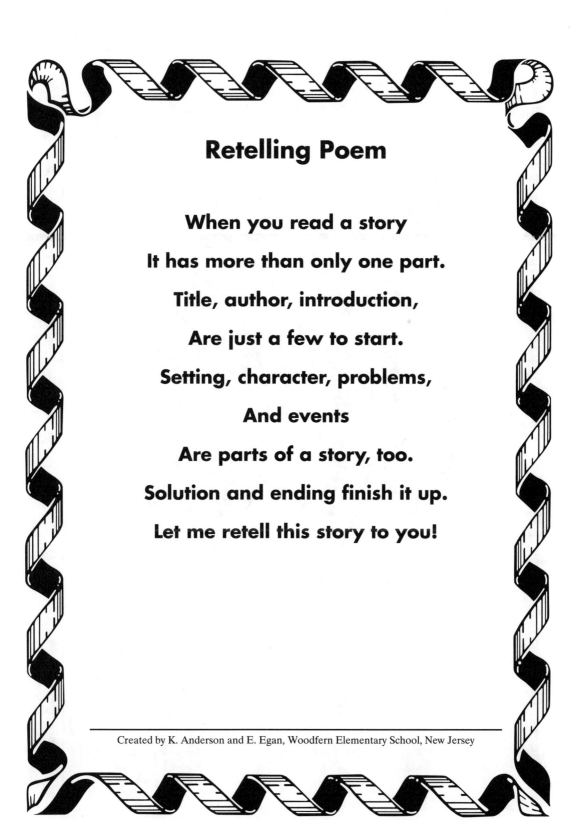

Retelling Poem

When you read a story

It has more than only one part.

Title, author, introduction,

Are just a few to start.

Setting, character, problems,

And events

Are parts of a story, too.

Solution and ending finish it up.

Let me retell this story to you!

Created by K. Anderson and E. Egan, Woodfern Elementary School, New Jersey

Directions: Color and cut out! Keep this someplace handy and use it to guide you when retelling a story.

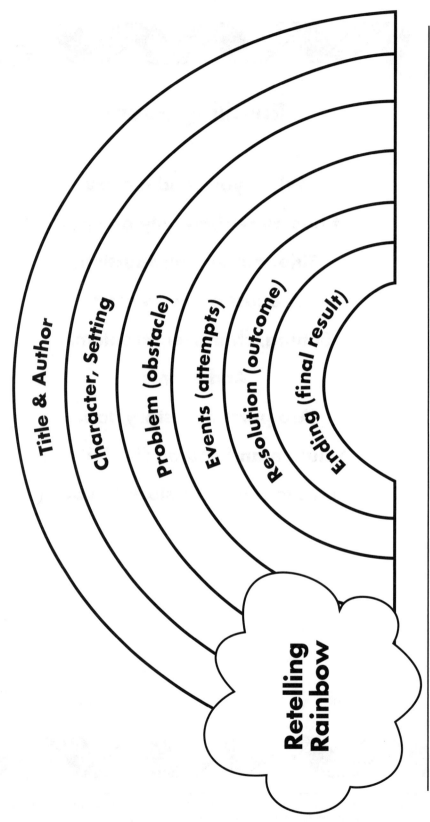

Title & Author

Character, Setting

Problem (obstacle)

Events (attempts)

Resolution (outcome)

Ending (final result)

Retelling Rainbow

"Tell Me a Story": Developmentally Appropriate Retelling Strategies by Jill Hansen. Copyright © 2004 by the International Reading Association. May be copied for classroom use.

Story Elements Rubric

Name _____ **Date** _____

Book Title _____

Score 1 point for each story element included.

Setting	**Where**	_____
	When	_____
Characters	**Main**	_____
	Others	_____
Problem		_____
Events	**#1**	_____
	#2	_____
	#3	_____
Solution		_____
Ending		_____
Total Score		_____

Comments:

Graphic Organizers for Fluent Retelling Level

Plot Summary Map

Character's goal

Obstacle

Attempt 1	**Attempt 2**	**Attempt 3**

Outcome 1	**Outcome 2**	**Outcome 3**

Resolution

Ending

If additional attempts occur use back of page.

Plot Summary Rubric

Name _____   **Date** _____

Book Title _____

Author _____

Directions: To determine the score for attempts to reach the goal, divide the attempts mentioned by the actual number of attempts, and carry the fractional answer over to the Total column.

Did the summary include   Total

• **Statement of the character's goal?**   _____

• **Obstacle preventing goal attainment?**   _____

• **Attempts to reach goal/outcome of each?**   _____
  (number of attempts mentioned/actual attempts ___/___)

• **Attempts in proper sequence?**   _____

• **Outcome of final event?**   _____

• **A statement about what the character does
  or feels about the outcome?**   _____

Divide total by 6 and multiply by 100 to determine percentage _____

Written Plot Summary

Name _____

Book Title _____

Author _____

Directions: Answer the questions below in complete sentences.
Then, rewrite the answers in paragraph form to complete a written
plot summary.

1. **What was the character's goal?** _____

    _____

2. **What gets in the way of the character reaching this goal?** _____

    _____

3. **What was the first attempt?** _____

    _____

4. **What was the first outcome?** _____

    _____

5. **What was the second attempt?** _____

    _____

6. **What was the second outcome?** _____

    _____

(continued)

Written Plot Summary (continued)

7. **What was the third attempt?** _____

_____

8. **What was the third outcome?**_____

_____

9. **What was the final attempt and outcome?** _____

_____

10. **What did the character do or how did the character feel about
the final outcome?** _____

_____

Rewrite the plot summary below by combining your answers.

_____

_____

_____

_____

_____

_____

_____

_____

_____

_____

Advanced Story Map

Name _____

Book Title _____ Author _____

Main character's goal

Other characters

Obstacle

Episode 1

Episode 2

Episode 3

(Add additional episodes on back, as needed.)

Setting
Where

When

Resolution

Ending

Retelling Rubric

Name_____ **Date** _____

Book Title/Author_____

Directions: Assign 1 point to each story element mentioned. If the element requires multiple answers, adjust the points accordingly. Then, total the points and divide by 10. Multiply by 100 to obtain a percentage.

Type of Retelling (Circle one)

Guided   Unguided   Oral   Written

Did the student

State the title?   _____

State the author?   _____

Describe the setting?
(where and when)   _____

State the characters?   _____

Name all the characters?   _____

State the problem?   _____

State the events?   _____

Retell the events in sequence?   _____

Give solution to problem?   _____

Tell how the story ended?   _____

Total score _____/10

Comments:

References

Brown, H., & Cambourne, B. (1987). *Read and retell: A strategy for the whole language/ natural learning classroom*. Portsmouth, NH: Heinemann.

Carbo, M. (1996). Whole language vs. phonics: The great debate. *Principal, 75*, 36–38.

Clay, M.M. (1993). *An observation survey of early literacy achievement*. Portsmouth, NH: Heinemann.

Cutting, B. (1992). *Getting started in whole language: The complete guide for every teacher*. Bothell, WA: Wright Group.

Fountas, I.C., & Pinnell, G.S. (1996). *Guided reading: Good first teaching for all children*. Portsmouth, NH: Heinemann.

Fountas, I.C., & Pinnell, G.S. (1999). *Matching books to readers: Using leveled books in guided reading, K–3*. Portsmouth, NH: Heinemann.

Glazer, S.M., & Brown, C.S. (1993). *Portfolios and beyond: Collaborative assessment in reading and writing*. Norwood, MA: Christopher-Gordon.

Heiden, D.E. (1999). Assessing literacy learners: A tale of two children. In S.M. Blair-Larsen & K.A. Williams (Eds.), *The balanced reading program: Helping all students achieve success* (pp. 72–103). Newark, DE: International Reading Association.

International Reading Association (IRA) & National Association for the Education of Young Children (NAEYC). (1998). *Learning to read and write: Developmentally appropriate practices for young children*. Newark, DE: Author; Washington, DC: Author.

Johnson, D. (1999). Critical issue: Addressing the literacy needs of emergent and early readers. *Pathways to School Improvement*. Retrieved November 28, 2003, from http://www.ncrel.org/sdrs/issues.htm

McCarrier, A., Pinnell, G.S., & Fountas, I.C. (1999). *Interactive writing: How language and literacy come together, K–2*. Portsmouth, NH: Heinemann.

Morrow, L.M. (1993). *Literacy development in the early years: Helping children read and write* (2nd ed.). Englewood Cliffs, NJ: Prentice Hall.

National Institute of Child Health and Human Development. (2000). *Report of the National Reading Panel. Teaching children to read: An evidence-based assessment of the scientific research literature on reading and its implications for reading instruction* (NIH Publication No. 00-4769). Washington, DC: U.S. Government Printing Office.

Parkes, B. (2000). *Read it again! Revisiting shared reading*. Portland, ME: Stenhouse.

Routman, R. (1991). *Invitations: Changing as teachers and learners K–12*. Portsmouth, NH: Heinemann.

Routman, R. (2000). *Conversations: Strategies for teaching, learning, and evaluating*. Portsmouth, NH: Heinmann.

Spiegel, D. (1999). The perspective of the balanced approach. In S.M. Blair-Larsen & K.A. Williams (Eds.), *The balanced reading program: Helping all students achieve success* (pp. 8–23). Newark, DE: International Reading Association.

Stanovich, K.E. (1986). Matthew effects in reading: Some consequences of individual differences in the acquisition of literacy. *Reading Research Quarterly, 21*, 360–407.

Children's Literature References

Broekhuizen, R.H. (1990). *Something soft for Danny Bear*. Ill. M. Payne. Crystal Lake, IL: Rigby.

Davidson, A. (1993a). *How fire came to earth*. Ill. J. Wallner. Crystal Lake, IL: Rigby.

Davidson, A. (1993b). *How turtle raced beaver*. Ill. R. Parkinson. Crystal Lake, IL: Rigby.

Lang, G. (1996). *Washing our dog*. Littleton, MA: Sundance.

Minarik, E.H. (1984). *A kiss for Little Bear*. Ill. M. Sendak. New York: HarperTrophy.

Neitzel, S. (1989). *The jacket I wear in the snow*. Ill. N. Winslow Parker. New York: Scholastic.

Nelson, J. (1989). *There's a dragon in my wagon*. Ill. M. Anthony. Cleveland, OH: Modern Curriculum Press.

Parker, J. (1989). *Emma's problem*. Ill. S. Cammell. Crystal Lake, IL: Rigby.

Pollock, Y. (1994). *The old man's mitten: A Ukrainian tale*. Ill. T. Hill. Greenvale, NY: Mondo.

Roop, P.G., & Roop, C. (1987). *Keep the lights burning, Abbie*. Ill. P.E. Hanson. Minneapolis, MN: Carolrhoda.

Shilling, T. (1997). *Mr. McCready's cleaning day*. Ill. S.M. King. New York: Scholastic.

Sloan, P., & Sloan, S. (1994). *At the farm*. Ill. G. Weiss. Littleton, MA: Sundance.

Sloan, P., & Sloan, S. (1995). *A tree fell over the river*. Ill. T. Culkin-Lawrence. Littleton, MA: Sundance.

Sloan, P., & Sloan, S. (1996). *Colors*. Littleton, MA: Sundance.

Titherington, J. (1986). *Pumpkin, pumpkin*. New York: Greenwillow.

Index

Note: Page numbers followed by *f* indicate figures.

A

B

C

D